LITTLE SECRET BIG DREAMS

PINK AND BROWN IN THE WHITE HOUSE

[handwritten inscription]

MOE VELA

MOtivational PRESS
LEADERS IN GLOBAL PUBLISHING

Published by Motivational Press, Inc.
1777 Aurora Road
Melbourne, Florida, 32935
www.MotivationalPress.com

Manufactured in the United States of America.

ISBN: 978-1-62865-321-2

CONTENTS

DEDICATION

I dedicate this book to my parents. They have been my rock, my anchor and my compass in life. It is their unconditional love, their wisdom and their example that has been the foundation upon which I have built my amazing journey. I just simply love you.

FOREWORD

THERE ARE THOSE TIMES IN LIFE WHEN WORDS ARE JUST
simply inadequate to describe our most intimate and profound thoughts and emotions. I will make a valiant attempt to
use words to share my story. I write this book in hope that maybe one kid somewhere will choose life over suicide, that one person will be inspired to live their truth and that we will all love
more freely, laugh more often and celebrate the gift of life each
and every day.

As a young, gay, Hispanic, Catholic kid growing up in south
Texas, I never dreamed that I would one day make American
history as the first gay American and the first Hispanic American to serve twice in the White House in a senior executive role.
Rather than continue to ask "why me," I have decided to share
my story out of an abundance of gratitude. There has been much
turmoil along the way and many joyful memories. I share many
of them in this book—the good, bad and the ugly.

I am confident and clear that, although my chance to make
a little bit of American history was overwhelmingly meaningful to me personally, my story is no more special nor exciting

than anyone else's. I was given a gift—the gift of being exposed to first-hand experiences and people that most will never see or know. There is not a day that goes by that I am not eternally grateful for the straw I drew. I'm not better nor different; I was just given a unique perch, platform, perspective and point of view. The soul-searching of my youth and the eventual ability to live my truth and my miniscule foray into American history have allowed me to recognize that it is through vulnerability, honesty and keeping it real that we honor and celebrate our shared humanity.

I share my story so that a few more people will get a more personal and intimate look into the lives of two of our nation's most incredible public servants—Al Gore and Joe Biden. My experiences in service to them and our nation have impacted my life in immeasurable ways.

I look in the mirror each day and see a flawed human being who is making his best effort to improve and evolve, but I have resigned myself to the premise that my story might help one person to live a fuller and more enriched life if they could learn from my mistakes. It's worth sharing my story if just one life lesson inspires and motivates someone to shoot for the stars and follow their dreams. For it is making myself vulnerable through the truth that makes me human, just like each of you. There will be those who will judge or criticize me, but I write this for all those who feel different, struggle with their insecurities, choose to love and be loved, believe in humanity, support the exchange of positive energy and know that at the end of the day we are all equal. This one's for you!

CHAPTER ONE

O N OCTOBER 23, 1961, AFTER ABOUT 16 HOURS OF LABOR, I entered this world at 8 pounds, 10 ounces. Clearly I have battled weight issues ever since! I was born at Valley Baptist Medical Center in Harlingen, Texas, where, coincidentally today my brother is the CEO.

Let's start at the very beginning... a very good place to start!

I was fortunate to be born into a pioneer family in the southern tip of Texas. We call this area of Texas the Rio Grande Valley because it is bordered on the east by the Gulf of Mexico, the western boundary ends near a city called Rio Grande City, a few smaller cities make up the northern boundary and the Rio Grande River and the Mexican border make up the southern boundary of my home area. Due to its proximity to the Mexican border, the area has been and continues to be predominantly Hispanic.

On the Vela side of the family, I was born into a family that settled in the Rio Grande Valley in the mid-1800s. The Vela family has a long and rich history in the Valley, as the family ranch once consisted of thousands of acres which housed its own school, church and several homesteads. The Laguna Seca Ranch, as it is known, meaning "dry lagoon," houses the Vela Family Cemetery, where many of my ancestors dating back to the 1800s are resting in peace.

Blessed to be born into a pioneer family

It was on this swath of Texas ranch land that the Vela family began what has been over a century and a half of contributions to the Rio Grande Valley. Family lore and Texas history books have it that on an otherwise normal day at the Laguna Seca Ranch, my great-great aunt, Carlota Vela, and my great-great grandfather, Macedonio Vela, welcomed a Spanish visiting missionary to the ranch, which was customary at that time.

Macedonio Vela

Macedonio Vela—the patriarch

It was not uncommon for these visiting priests to conduct a Catholic Mass at the Laguna Seca Ranch on their way through. What remains today of that church on the ranch are four walls covered with brush (if walls could talk). On this particular day in 1871 the Spanish missionary is said to have been carrying a small pouch filled with some seeds. Generations of Velas have ensured that each of us is fully aware that the missionary recognized that the rich, clay-like red soil of the Laguna Seca Ranch would be a conducive environment for the seeds to grow. The missionary blessed the seeds, as we are told, and asked my great-great aunt, Carlota Vela, to plant them on the ranch. The missionary must have had a premonition, divine intervention or just a good eye for agriculture, as those seeds he had brought with him from Spain were Valencia oranges, and the Vela family and the Laguna Seca Ranch became the fathers and birthplace (I often say "mothers" because the seeds were given to my great-great aunt) of citrus in the state of Texas. There are many who argue that our family and the family ranch are the birthplace of citrus in the entire United States, but Florida has long debated that point. Regardless, on October 23, 1961, I was born into a family that had long before made an indelible mark on the history of the great state in which I was born.

Unbeknownst to me, being born a Vela came with expectations, responsibilities and a tremendous sense of pride and honor. My great-great grandfather, Macedonio Vela, was the patriarch of what today numbers well over 8,000 descendants who can trace their roots to him. He and my great-great grandmother were the proud parents of eight children, and the Hispanic Catholic tradition of reproduction took over from there.

One of those eight children was my great grandfather, Macedonio Vela. And one of his nine children was my grandfather, Roberto Vela. I was fortunate to get to know my grandfather for the first several years of my life. My recollections of him as a child are of his routine visits to the local bar, The Three Palms, where he would walk and consume a fair share of Budweisers on a daily basis. My grandmother, Maria Luisa, as I have been told, was angelic and faced an untimely death in her early forties on the steps of the Immaculate Heart of Mary Catholic Church in Harlingen, Texas. She was originally from Monterrey, Nuevo Leon, Mexico. Until recent years, as we passed a landmark in our hometown of Harlingen, Texas, my father would relay the same story that was etched in his memory bank about how his mother passed away at the door to the original hospital in our hometown because the Anglos would not allow her entry because she was of Mexican heritage. Donald Trump's ridiculous and incendiary racist comments about "Mexicans" in this past election were personal to our family—it breaks my heart to see that some things have not changed.

My grandmother left a gift to the world in the nine children she bore. In writing this chapter, I now realize the number nine seems to have special meaning to the Vela family; you would think it would be my roulette number, but it has been 33 for years, and that might explain my consistent gambling losses. My grandfather, Roberto, was a self-taught man with a curious grin. I vividly remember my parents taking my siblings and I over to his house on a very routine basis, as it was not but a few miles from our family home in Harlingen. Engrained in my mind is the image of my grandfather sitting in his wooden chair that my father made for him—it was white and what today we would describe as an Adirondack chair.

I think they just thought of it as Buelito Vela's (as we referred to him in Spanish and which was short for Abuelito or grandfather) chair. All I know is that he inevitably had a Budweiser in one hand and was able to hug each of us as we arrived without spilling a drop of his beer. I remember his scent—it was that unique smell of someone who has consumed several beers mixed with his aftershave. He had a head of pure white hair, and it was cut as a crew cut or flat top. One of my memories of Buelito Vela was the feel of his stubble as he held our faces to his cheeks to kiss our foreheads. Kissing and hugging are strong cultural traditions in Hispanic families, and I kiss my father each and every time I see him, as I watched him kiss his father until the day he died.

My grandfather had made a fateful decision many years before, as had many of his siblings and cousins, to leave the Laguna Seca Ranch and start their families in other parts of the Rio Grande Valley, the State of Texas and across the nation and the world. My grandfather chose a little town in the central eastern part of the Rio Grande Valley called Harlingen, Texas, as I have previously mentioned.

My grandparents' nine children were Teresa de Jesus, Eva Feliciana, Maria Luisa, Roberto II , Moises Vicente, Antonio Humberto, Filemon Bartholome, Patricio Delfino Carlos Flavio Vela. My dad, tios and tias (uncles and aunts in Spanish) were born on a dirt floor in a small house on B Street. As my father tells it, my grandfather was a laborer and my grandmother was a housewife, so they were poor from an economic perspective but rich in love and spirit. Their toys consisted of old socks that were filled with any natural filler from the yard to form a ball, and many of their meals consisted of large vats of tamales and meals such as beans, rice and tortillas—culinary endeavors that were relatively inexpensive and could feed an army.

Dad and his father and brothers, circa 1958
From L-R: Roberto, Filemon, Buelito Vela, Patricio, Carlos,
Moises (my father) and Antonio seated in front

Tragically, during my father's sixteenth year of life, his mother died on the steps of Immaculate Heart of Mary Catholic Church after Mass; she devoutly attended on a weekly if not daily basis. Over the years, I have had many discussions with my father, and as many men of his generation, he is not one to speak of emotions, but it has always been evident to me that my grandmother's passing left a tragic void in my dad's life, as in the lives of his siblings. Their Tia Eva, from Monterrey, Mexico (my grandmother's sister) stepped in and became a surrogate mother to the nine Vela children. Some of my fondest memories in my youth were going to Monterrey, Mexico and visiting "Buelita Eva," as we called her, and staying in the guest rooms of her home in the heart of Monterrey. Her house was something I had never seen or experienced before, and it was always a treat to stay in bedrooms that opened into a center open-air courtyard and listen to her parrots chirping as morning came upon us. There always seemed to be a brisk breeze and coolness when we were there, and it brought me some sense of comfort. On our trips to Monterrey to visit Buelita Eva, we would never fail to go around the corner and eat consommé de pollo (chicken broth) with tortillas—I will never forget the confusion in my youthful mind as to how a fried tortilla could be orange!

With the absence of my grandmother, my grandfather was relegated to finish raising his brood of nine children on his own. In addition to the support and assistance from Buelita Eva, my father's two older sisters were forced to give up their career ambitions and dreams to help raise their six younger brothers. The oldest Vela sibling, my Tia Tere, suffered rheumatic fever at the age of 3 or 4, and in those days the medical advancements were limited, such that she suffered irreparable brain damage and lived the rest of her life with the mental capacity of an adolescent. To this day, we fondly remember her as the angel in the Vela family, and it taught us a sense of compassion and respect for those with disabilities from an early age.

It was Tia Eva and Tia Licha (Licha is a common nickname for the name Maria Luisa) who raised their brothers—as I had the blessing of knowing them both until they passed, it was their dedication to their brothers and their mentally disabled sister that was my first glimpse of the meaning of "familia." It was those two aunts who hosted every family Easter egg hunt and filled the eggs with quarters and sometimes dollars. And it was they who unselfishly lined the Christmas tree with gifts for each of their beloved 16 nephews and nieces. Their examples of family unity and the value of family set the foundation upon which all of us practice to this day.

My Tia Eva became the matriarch of the family. My grandfather had gone from being a day laborer to owning his own small business and it was Tia Eva who took over my grandfather's neighborhood bookkeeping service, Vela Bookkeeping. (Ironically, I went to law school because there was no math or science—I'm not sure how I missed that bookkeeping gene!) Regrettably, unlike a few of my siblings, I didn't pick up my Tia Eva's financial management prowess, as she would save every loose dime, penny and nickel until she had enough to take her sisters on a trip or buy a piano or a new car. In hindsight, it was utterly amazing that through frugality and a thrifty spirit, she turned her business into a successful venture and gave us all our first example of the value of being good stewards of our money and the benefits of hard work.

Dad's sisters from L-R: Teresa, Eva and Maria Luisa

As my aunts and grandfather struggled to make ends meet and feed these growing boys, they were also being taught that education was the key to success and the key to a fulfilling life. Although uneducated himself, my grandfather knew that for his boys to lead a better life than his, they had to receive an education. I am reminded of the story that although my grandfather was a day laborer and later opened Vela Bookkeeping Services, he would be damned if his children were not going to be given the same opportunities that other kids were given—it was then that he fought the Harlingen School Board when his children were denied the ability to attend an all-Anglo Stephen F. Austin Elementary School because of their Hispanic ethnicity. As fate would have it, the uneducated father of nine not only opened the doors of that school for his children, but it was precisely where my four siblings and I spent our elementary school years some 30 years or so later. Many things had changed between the tenures of the two sets of Vela children at that school, but some things had not. When my siblings and I attended Stephen F. Austin Elementary, we were not allowed to speak Spanish on the playground, but thanks to my grandfather, we were otherwise there with equal opportunity and access. More on those formative years later.

In many ways, my grandfather's fierce defense of equality, family and education set the stage for the passion and dedication of many Velas to this day to be a voice for the voiceless, fight for inclusion of the disenfranchised, never stop advocating for civil rights and be of service to our communities and our nation. My grandfather, my father and his siblings were tremendous role models in planting a seed in all of us that we must never forget from where we come. It all started on that dirt floor for them, so no matter how much financial success any of us achieves, no matter what title is bestowed on any one of us or no matter how famous one might become, that dirt floor is a reminder to us all that we are all equal in the eyes of our Beholder. Humility and service are the Vela way.

I remain in awe that a self-taught man such as my grandfather was insightful and visionary enough to know that his children needed an education—he must have known that with that spark they would one day make a difference in the lives of many. With that start, three of the Vela brothers became attorneys, two educators and one a public servant. As I previously shared, my Tia Eva worked tirelessly to become a successful small business owner, and my Tia Licha went back to school later in life to become a nurse.

In addition to the tremendous examples set by my father and my uncles and aunts, the fact that my father and four of his brothers served our nation in the military makes my heart burst with pride. I am equally proud of the courage and sacrifice my aunts made for their brothers—that example of unselfishness and dedication to family will be at my core until my final breath. As I reflect on what my aunts did for their siblings, the seeds planted by my great-great aunt and the beautiful example of my mother that you will subsequently learn about, it is no accident that I consider myself a feminist. I have seen the role of strong, fierce and courageous women on my journey, and I will fight for their equality until they no longer need my advocacy.

My father had a distinguished career as an attorney for over 50 years in the Rio Grande Valley. As an attorney myself, it is my father's example that guides my every step and move. It was common at the Vela dinner table for any of my siblings and I to ask why Dad brought home a baby alligator, a bushel of tomatoes, a puppy or a piece of jewelry. Every day that my father practiced law, he demonstrated and redefined the meaning of pro bono. We watched him serve the poor with the same vigor and dedication with which he served his paying clients. It was a sense of pride for his clients, Dad would explain to us, that they be able to give him something as compensation. Whether it was a pet for his children, something from their farm or garden or just prayers and good wishes, I watched my father accept them with a deep sense of appreciation, always ensuring that the client knew he was touched by their gesture. In hindsight, one of the many lessons I learned from this experience was that of empathy with dignity and respect. Daddy taught me to empathize with those less fortunate and in a more challenging station in life, but he never ever patronized them.

Of my father's siblings, it was my Tio Filemon, or Judge Vela, as most people know him, who also greatly impacted my thinking and perspective. In the middle of President Jimmy Carter's administration, President Carter bestowed a tremendous honor onto the Vela family and appointed my uncle a United States Federal Judge in the southern district of Texas, which is within the Fifth Circuit. He was one of the first handful of Hispanic Federal judges in the nation, and he served with distinction and notoriety until he lost a battle with stomach cancer. He rose to the rank of Senior Judge and was a fair and impartial jurist who managed his courtroom with respect and decorum. Several years ago, the Vela family was once again honored when the Federal Courthouse in Brownsville, Texas was co-named after my uncle. There was probably no greater thrill in law school then studying one of your own uncle's rulings and cases—I am so fortunate.

It is estimated that there are well over 10,000 Vela descendants from Macedonio Vela currently living around the world

As part of the Vela legacy, many generations of south Texans will be able to learn about my uncle and my father and their immense contributions to the Valley when they see the two middle schools named in their honor. It is quite fun throughout the year when Filemon B. Vela Middle School in Brownsville plays or competes against Moises V. Vela Middle School in Harlingen. You can only imagine the jest and exchanges between my brother and I and our cousins, Filemon Jr. and Ralph.

I know that I am eternally grateful to my aunts for giving my father the opportunity to become the man he is, and I recognize that without that foundation of their sacrifice, this journey of mine would not have been possible.

My father and his siblings were raised devoutly Catholic because of my grandmother's deep and abiding faith, a faith that continues to be my father's moral compass to this day. Even with the advancement of Alzheimer's and dementia, Daddy's devotion to the Virgin Virgen Mary provides him solace and strength. During my visits home to South Texas, I often find Dad praying the rosary or reminding us all to pray—I don't share my father's religious beliefs, but I profoundly admire his faith, and we certainly share the same convictions and principles. I hope each day of my life that I am half the man my father is, and I am eternally grateful to him for instilling in me those principles of integrity, honesty, respect, dignity and service, to always act with compassion and empathy for those less fortunate. Regrettably, as I write this book, we had to place my father in a nursing care facility. At 86, the ravages of dementia and Alzheimer's have taken their toll. I am amazed that even though he might not recall what he ate for breakfast, he still loves every minute of every day. I have never met another human being like him in his ability to truly seize the moment. All of my life, like my siblings, we have tried to spend as much quality time with our parents as possible, and, in my case, that involved trips to the Mediterranean, the Vatican, Colorado, San Diego, Birmingham, Washington, D.C., the Caribbean and many others. Without exception, I watched and listened with amazement as my father genuinely thought and expressed that every dirt road, mountain, waterfall, sunrise, moonlight, relic, museum, artifact, stalk of corn, blade of grass and person he met was the best he had ever seen, smelled, heard or experienced. Thanks to my father and his spirit, I would argue that "carpe diem" is a Spanish phrase!

I share all of this family history because it is the foundation of who I am. I don't think we can understand a person nor their plight without understanding their roots. It is my roots that have instilled in me my core values, commitment to service, love of life and the fundamental understanding that we are called to leave this world a little better than we found it.

The man I admire the most in life—my father, Moises Vela

CHAPTER TWO

THE VELA SIDE OF THE EQUATION IS ONLY HALF, AS WE ALL know! I was carried in the womb of the mostwonderful woman I have ever known by the name of Maria Josefa Mendoza Vela. It was she who endured the 16 hours of labor and played cards with my father and our family doctor, Doctor John Dieck, until I finally decided to make my entrance. Anyone who knows me well knows I take my entrances pretty seriously and rarely quietly—I am told it all started on that debut.

My beloved mother is in so many ways a traditional Hispanic mother of that generation, yet in so many ways she broke the mold. She is reverent in her faith and prayerful, yet irreverent with a wicked sense of humor. She was protective like most moms and always concerned about the well-being of her children but gave us the freedom to explore, adventure and make mistakes. She was strong and decisive and needed no belt, as her hand would leave a welt to be remembered, but she is the epitome of unconditional love. Above and beyond all else, it is from her that I got my gift of laughter—she taught us it was okay to find humor in even the worst of circumstances, not to ever take ourselves too seriously and giggling was healthy.

Unfortunately, Catholic Mass on Sunday was not exempt from the Vela giggles—and it raised my father's hackles like nothing else. A great example is when my father's oldest sister, Tia Eva, who suffered from the same propensity to battle her weight that I do, literally waddled off the altar with about 200 hosts in her Eucharistic minister chalice. Regrettably, she miscalculated the step and the hosts (which Catholics believe have been converted to the body of Christ at that point in the Mass) went rolling all over the cement floor as far as ten rows back. The more we tried to control ourselves, the more severe the giggles became. Our fearless leader, our mother, led the way. Just imagine, 200 baby Jesuses rolling on the floor! It got so bad that my father kicked us out of Mass. It wasn't the first nor the last time that under my mother's tutelage, we laughed our way into or out of a situation.

I recall attending another Mass many years later in the city of sin, Las Vegas. Yes, even in Las Vegas, the Velas would attend Mass. Only my mother would be able to drop a bucket with $500 of quarters during the priest's sermon on the Las Vegas strip. Unfortunately for her, after the laughter died down, the priest was quick to ask the parishioners to please pick them up and put them in the collection basket, ruining my mom's plan to play them after Mass at Circus Circus. As my mom so aptly said, "The good Lord had other plans, I guess".

My mother was born in the central part of the Rio Grande Valley in a small town called Donna, Texas and was later raised in an idyllic town on the Laguna Madre Bay called Port Isabel, Texas. My siblings and I are very fortunate in that we had three abuelitas (grandmothers) and not just the traditional two. Mama Estefana (as we called her), my mother's birth mother, became deathly ill upon delivering my mother, so her sister-in-law, Buelita Pepa, and her husband, Manuel Mendoza, raised my mother. Upon reaching her teenage years, she was given the chance to pick which family to live with, and she chose to stay with her aunt and uncle.

The beauty is that we were taught no distinction between Buelita Pepa and Mama Estefana—it was all familia, and the love bond with my mother's siblings, Mama Estefana and my Yanez cousins was and is as strong as can be. My mother had four natural-born sisters and one brother—my Tias Noemi, Lucilla, Christina (Tina) and Yolanda (Yoli), and Uncle Dan.

Mom with two of her surviving siblings—Yoli Chapa and Lucy Tisdale. She also has a sister, Tina Acevedo and her brother, Dan Yanez, who are also living. Their sister, Noemi, is deceased.

We often joke with my mother because she was very quick to teach us as youngsters that she was the valedictorian of her class at Port Isabel High School—when we finally reached an age of understanding, we figured out that it was a class of eight! The reality is that my mother was and is a brilliant woman. She was teaching piano lessons in her teenage years, cheerleading for the Port Isabel Tarpons AND busy becoming valedictorian.

As a way of teaching us the virtues of chastity and morality, my mom would often tell us as we reached our teenage years that she was so innocent, pure and chaste that when she finally made out with my father under the water tower outside of the city limits of Port Isabel, she thought she was pregnant. For years, we listened and admired the innocence represented in the story. It wasn't until I fully comprehended the facts of life that I realized that if she thought she could get pregnant by kissing my father, what the hell was she doing making out?

One of the stories that most inspires me about my mother's upbringing was the commitment, desire and conviction she possessed for education. After attending her first year or two of classes in Brownsville, Texas, at Texas Southmost Junior College which entailed a 30-minute ride from Port Isabel in each direction, Mom knew she had to go elsewhere to finish her Bachelor's degree. She enrolled at Texas A & I in Kingsville, Texas (today it is Texas A & M Kingsville and represented by my cousin, Filemon Vela, in the United States Congress). This required my grandparents to drive my mother 95 miles in each direction several times per week so she could continue her studies. I often ponder about how many of us would do that today.

Family lore has it that one day as my mother wandered across the campus of Texas A & I University, she encountered the school mascot who had escaped from its pen, and it chased her up a tree. The school mascot was and remains a javalina, which is a pecuniary or wild boar with tusks. They are not attractive and snort loudly—you can imagine the fun we have had with that story over the years.

Mother's upbringing, as she has shared with us, was in a very disciplined household. I think it helped my mom a great deal that her adopted sister, Helen, bordered on incorrigible and created a constant distraction. I am confident that my mom was as studious and obedient as she says she was, but even the best of children welcome parental distraction.

Abuelito Mendoza, Mom's uncle and adopted father, I am told, was a gentle soul. He is remembered as being wicked smart, a man of few words, cerebral and calm. He enjoyed tranquility, and in his moments of solitude, he invented many interesting products. There are several patents registered in his name. My Buelita Pepa, my mom's aunt and adopted mother, was an educator and was the disciplinarian in the family. She was gentle but stern. Serious but loving. My grandfather actually passed away when I was just a few years old from tuberculosis, and I was blessed that my Buelita Pepa lived with us until her passing when I was around fifteen years of age. As is the tradition in many Hispanic families, our elders of that generation lived with us until their death if at all possible—another example of the importance and value placed on familia in the Latino culture.

I fondly remember the many times she would hand my brother and I a fifty-cent piece after our pee-wee football games that she had saved from her social security check. I also remember how her demeanor changed at home if one of us took cookies from her cookie jar or anything from her refrigerator without permission. It was a scary way to learn respect for our elders and for that which is not ours, but it worked. It was a little different than the traditional Latino way to teach a child—the use of the dreaded "chancla"(sandal).

It is not uncommon to hear me tell the story of Buelita Pepa's funeral, as it was probably the first funeral in my life where I possessed the cognizance and understanding of the finality of life. My recollection is of my brother, Manny, and I crying uncontrollably at her casket because we remembered knocking her down several years before as we played football in the living room one lazy day. I guess in some crazy way we thought that the fall several years earlier was linked to her death!

It was clear that my mother had learned much from her parents, and every day she has been on this Earth, she has imparted her wisdom and love upon us. I admire and respect so many things about my incredible mother, but one near the top of the list is her ability to be a well-rounded and balanced woman. This woman has never failed to treat each of her children equally, has never failed to love us unconditionally and truly gave us a judgment-free zone to call home. My mother continues to demonstrate that a woman can be a caring mother, a dutiful wife and a woman of deep and abiding faith, hunt for deer and fish in the Laguna Madre by day and host a party for 200 that same evening. She is truly remarkable and has never neglected her duties or responsibilities to so many of us.

I have never met another woman like her--my beautiful mom

Like my father, my mother is a woman of faith. We speak daily, and on those few days of the month that I am across the world or just forget to call, she knows how to turn on the Latina Catholic guilt and can rival any Jewish mother on that front. I am convinced that it is not that she didn't get to hear my voice, but it is a day when she cannot remind me that she had prayed for me in her morning prayers or thought of me during her daily devotional or as she prayed the rosary. I truly admire the purity of her faith. As I often tell her in our daily calls, I may not agree or share that same faith, but I appreciate the prayers and good will. We have come to have a mutual understanding and respect for each other when it comes to religion. Mom has finally realized that my spirituality is so special to me. She now understands the distinction between being religious and spiritual. It disappoints her to know that I find religious institutions and organizations generally offensive, destructive, divisive and judgmental, but she knows that I live my life with a solid core of love, respect and compassion, the virtues and values that she and Dad taught at us at every turn, in every way and by every word or deed.

Perhaps the greatest example my mother has taught us is in her devotion to my father. After 61 years of marriage, she still looks at him with endearing eyes and kisses him with what I imagine was the same fervor as under the water tower. I don't know that I will ever see a love story like theirs again. It is truly the root of my romanticism, and, after two failed relationships, I wish I had taken more lessons from them on how to create an enduring love story.

It never failed that my mom's gift of laughter took place at the most inopportune times. As a young man growing up in Texas, one of your rites of passage to all-out Texas manhood is when your father lets you finally hitch your family boat to the truck in preparation for one of your frequent fishing trips to the Laguna Madre. On this particular sunny south Texas day, since my brother, Manny, and I are only 15 months apart (poor Mom), Daddy asked us both to work in tandem and to go out and prepare the boat for departure. We were both beaming with pride as we manually rolled the boat about 2 feet and used all of our undeveloped muscles to lift the boat over the truck hitch. We had watched our father on dozens of occasions and had listened for several years to his meticulous instructions on how to properly hitch the boat. We heard the necessary sound that is made when the hitch engages; we jointly pulled up on the boat trailer to ensure it was safely in place and placed the safety pin in its proper location. With the pride only teenage boys can demonstrate, we announced to our father that the Mary Jo (the boat was named after our mother) was ready to go.

He led us back out to the truck with confidence and faith in our abilities, and off we went on our weekly fishing trip. About halfway through our small city of Harlingen, Manny and I looked to the left and sheepishly announced to Dad that the Mary Jo was riding alongside the truck and was starting to actually veer away from us and across the oncoming traffic at the Gibson's parking lot. Gibson's was a precursor to a Wal-mart, so the parking lot was filled with cars and pedestrians strolling to their vehicles. Manny and I began to engage in what our mom would have wanted us to do and taught us to do—we burst out in bellowing laughter that turned to nervous giggles and then fearful cackling. My father blew a gasket, and I will not quote his vocabulary at that moment. Fortunately, the Mary Jo missed all the oncoming traffic and missed every car in the parking lot and finished her untethered journey in a grassy lot. My brother and I fondly recall that incident to this day, and the giggles and laughter return, but we learned a great deal as well. First and foremost, that humor is important, but when there is a risk of life and damage to others or their property, humor has to wait. It was a lesson of maturity. And, we learned that pride carries a risk and can be dangerous!

It was my mother who taught me a sense of self and the value of developing a core. A core that stood for something, reflected my values and was my compass in life. I vividly remember a time in my youth when the Anglo children at our elementary school called me a "Meskin" (Mexican) which is equivalent to the "N" word in discrimination. I came home from school that day to tell my mother that I was not a Mexican-American—rather, I was just an American. My mother was perplexed but reacted swiftly as she told me in Spanish, "Eres tan Mexicano que tienes un calendario Azteca en el fundio." That translates to, "You are so Mexican that you have an Aztec calendar in your a*#*hole!" Mother was not trying to be vulgar, but her point has stayed with me to this day—I am proud of my heritage and even more proud to be an American.

I admire my mother profoundly, as I have watched her quietly and without fanfare hold the hand of a dying friend, pray with those less fortunate, hug thousands, inspire even more through her grace and warmth and teach and impact hundreds of young students who are today contributing adults in our society. Mother taught hundreds of young people in over 25 years in the classroom. Off and on throughout my childhood, Mom was an elementary school teacher, and I would watch her patience and energy in awe. She would romp and play with her kindergarteners, dance like she was on Dancing with the Stars, sing as if she was guest starring on the Lawrence Welk Show and make every child feel loved and special.

She possessed an ability in the classroom like she did at home—everyone feels loved in the presence of this magnificent woman. My mother as a teacher was an example for us all—I watched her quietly clothe her students when they came from poverty, feed and love them when they came from a broken home and hug them like she meant it no matter their color, social stratum or background. I strive every day of my life to always be myself, whether I'm with the president of the United States or the janitor at the law firm, and I strive to treat them exactly the same. I learned that from my parents.

It should have surprised none of us that at 81 years of age, my mother revealed that she was ready to live out one of her lifelong dreams. We immediately thought it might be a trip to Hawaii, owning her own slot machine or finding a fountain of eternal youth, but it was that she wanted to be a beauty queen. In typical Mary Jo Vela fashion, she set her heart and mind to it, and she was crowned Ms. Senior South Texas after her rendition of "New York, New York" brought down the house; she was ravishing in her evening gown. It is a memory and a picture I will never forget as I sat on the front row with my father, sisters and brother to cheer her on. It was yet another lesson that it is never too late to live one's dreams—patience and perseverance are tremendous virtues, and my mom is living proof. Possibly the cutest part of the experience for our family is that the coronation created a monster of sorts—Mom now wants to be buried in that damn crown!

*Mom in her crown—what an inspiration to follow your dreams,
no matter your age or station in life*

Familia is at the core of who I am. It is the foundation upon
which my life has been built. I know that I could just easily have
been born into poverty, in a remote desert or forced to face harsh
challenges. I don't take my blessings for granted. I know how
fortunate I was to be born into the Vela and Mendoza/Yanez
families. I strive every day to live up to the ideals and standards
of my ancestors and parents. I know that my fundamental values, attributes, convictions and sense of purpose on this journey
come from familia.

The most special lady in my life

She is my rock—I love you mom!

CHAPTER THREE

As with most Hispanic families, I was not alone as an offspring of Moises and Mary Jo Vela. There are five of us: my eldest sisters, Patricia Maria (Patsy) and Maria Luisa (Luti), then me, followed by my only brother, Manuel (Manny), and our youngest sister, Maria Josefa (Pepper). In so many ways our upbringing was a Latino version of *Leave It to Beaver*.

My siblings never seize to amaze me in the way they positively impact the lives of so many on a daily basis.
From L-R: Patsy, Luti, Pepper, Mom, Dad, Manny and Me

Our formative years were in so many ways a traditional Latino upbringing, where we celebrated our heritage at every turn. Pinatas at our birthday parties, the Posadas at Christmas where one of the Vela children was inevitably Joseph, Mary or one of the Three Kings, and we consumed a very traditional Hispanic diet—you know, tortillas, rice, beans, fideo, carne guisada, enchiladas and calabaza con pollo.

From as early as I can remember, we had a live-in nanny to help my parents in the upkeep of our family home and raising the five of us. Magda, our nanny since I was about 8 years old, is part of our family. Growing up, my mother would not allow us to use the "M" word (maid), because my mother felt it was demeaning and haughty, and Magda was our equal and played an integral role in our upbringing.

The only home I remember living in is the one we still call the family homestead, where my mother resides these 50-plus years later. The house is literally a city block long but bent at an angle and sits on almost one acre. When Daddy bought the house, he paid $23,000 for it. The back fence of our yard bordered on what seemed like thousands of acres of farmland but in reality was about 1,000 acres owned by Mr. Myers. His horses provided us with such entertainment as we often fed them over the back fence. Some of the backyard was dense with jungle-like mesquite trees and Texas shrubs—creating a young boy's dream playground for adventure and curiosity. I spent many hours of my youth picking and throwing china berries, building dirt hills with tunnels and playing king of the mountain at nearby canal banks and many games of hide and seek among the trees and woodlands.

It was about this time that I experienced the first inkling of my sexual orientation. My parents were supervisory and watchful of us yet struck a healthy balance in letting us develop through safe adventure, curiosity and experience. In one of those times that I was adventuring, it involved wrestling with the little guy next door. We were both about 5 years of age, and I vividly recall the feeling that I was aroused (or what a pre-adolescent youth considers arousal) by the physical interaction. Even in the mind of a 5-year-old Hispanic boy in south Texas, I knew to keep this feeling to myself—the shame, fear and anxiety that plagued me for years began at that very moment in time. My life would never be the same again.

Mother always dressed us neatly and cleanly. In hindsight, and after reviewing hundreds of family photos, I often joke with my mother that the horizontal stripes on my shirts in most pictures did not match with the vertical stripes on my pants or shorts. She had no idea, but she was completely violating the gay fashion manual!

Cute if I have to say so myself!

Mom was resourceful during Dad's early years in the practice of the law. What with five young children and dance classes, football and baseball gear, bikes and so much, Mom saved up Gold Stamps and S&H Green stamps. We never lacked for anything, but we were not spoiled either. In fact, my mom was resourceful and strategic with her brood. I remember when our new mall in Harlingen was having its grand opening. In those days, the concept of a mall was indoor shopping—long buildings and usually one story, certainly not the multi-level and fancy shopping malls of today. When one grows up in small-town America, the grand opening of the mall is an "event," and the Vela family was not going to miss it. My mother found out that management was going to be throwing paper plates off the roof of the mall to the crowd below and that those plates would have a denomination on them. If a patron caught the plate, they would win the denomination on that plate. My mother has and continues to be a strategic thinker, so she took advantage of her large family and spread us about 20 yards apart to improve our chances.

I was about 10 years old at the time, and I was placed in my spot and coached on how to eye the paper plate and follow its trajectory and ultimately to catch the damn thing. The day was slightly windy, and I caught my target in my eyes. The wind was playing havoc with this plate, and I could see pretty early on that it said $100 on it. In that day and for a 10-year-old, $100 was like a year of allowances. I wanted that plate. Even with some turbulence, the plate was coming right to my pudgy little hands. As I was about to grab the plate, one of only about three Asian men in Harlingen at the time literally picked me up and threw me headfirst into the trash barrel so he could get the $100 plate.

As a result of that childhood incident, to this day, I cannot be around Asian art, and run down Canal Street in New York City because I have a phobia of most things Asian. I will eat Asian food, but I have no interest in travelling to an Asian country. On top of it all, I am claustrophobic, and I am confident it was from drowning in that trash!

Mom and Dad always taught us good hygiene, respect for our bodies and the value of a good appearance. It was a beautiful childhood with annual vacations to the mountains of Colorado and many interesting stops along the way like Langtry, Texas and the home of Judge Roy Bean, Palo Duro Canyon and the "Texas" production in the panhandle of Texas, idyllic Ruidoso, New Mexico and the splendor and majesty of Rocky Mountain National Park. Colorado holds very special memories to our family, as it was there for at least 15 summers that we enjoyed Buckskin Joe's, the Royal Gorge, the cliff dwellings and the infamous train ride along the gorges between Durango and Silverton.

It was on one of those memorable annual vacations to Colorado that I remember seeing my first glimpse of a gay couple holding hands as they walked down the street in downtown Denver. I was so frightened as I sat in the back of our family station wagon—offended by the comments made in the car about how weird the couple was and sick to my stomach in fear that my secret would be discovered. Every year that passed, my attraction to males would grow stronger, and I would desperately try to find a way to express this profound feeling and attraction but was paralyzed with anxiety.

This "little secret" that I discovered during that fateful wrestling match was the beginning of a long, painful and ultimately successful odyssey. In my feeble little mind, I knew even then that everyone around me was not like that, that it was "wrong" and "different" and that I had to extinguish, avoid and deny this truth in order to survive. After all, it was Texas—the land of cowboys, football, hunting and fishing; I was Hispanic—the culture of machismo; and I was Catholic—the place where priests and the church denounce homosexuality as a sin. The cards were heavily stacked against me and weighed heavily on my heart, mind and soul.

From an early age, in hindsight, it was obvious that I was overly conscientious, introspective and thoughtful. As endearing as those traits are, they are equally destructive to a youthful mind. The first known manifestation of the effects of this "little secret" in my life occurred when I reached kindergarten. With very few exceptions, every morning when my mother would go drop us off at kindergarten before she went to teach at a local elementary school, I would cry uncontrollably and refuse to leave my mother's side or get out of the car. She would have to drive through a nearby wooded area so I could see a bunny rabbit or some other wildlife in order to get me to agree to be left at school.

Later in adulthood, I have had the privilege of discussing this behavior pattern with many experts—psychologists, sociologists and sexual orientation experts. I knew that the only two people who would love me no matter what were my parents. I knew I had this "little secret," and that made me different. By leaving my mother every morning and joining this group of children who were "normal" or not like me, it was like putting a small island in the middle of the sea. This emotional turmoil instilled in me a battle with anxiety that has permeated my journey consistently. Those days of loneliness and fear were the foundation of a low self-esteem for many years to come.

As I continued through my pre-pubescent years, I slowly developed and discovered the inner strength to "fake it" and to be the Texas boy I was supposed to be—I excelled at Little League Football as a star defensive end, was an all-star first baseman in baseball, got my first 22-caliber rifle at about 10 years of age, killed my first eight-point buck at around 13 years of age and caught hundreds of fish, gigged many a flounder and snared many a crab in the Laguna Madre. In spite of hiding my "little secret," I found my inner survivor and discovered a respite in and love for the outdoors, sports, competition and family.

Like a good Texas boy!

As if the "little secret" were not enough, at around the age of 6, the optometrist discovered that I suffered from amblyopia (lazy eye muscle) in my left eye. There is no cure, but in those days they tried to regenerate the non-functioning eye muscle by making me patch my good eye and stare into a light bulb for minutes at a time. This eye impediment just added another layer of complexity in my development of self. It meant I had to wear glasses to the first grade, so now being called "four eyes" at least detracted from and guarded the "little secret" that no one could know.

Today I am a man of tremendous self-confidence who believes in himself and is comfortable in his own skin but transparently owns and battles his insecurities each and every day. It will come as a shock to most that my grade school years were an anxiety-ridden nightmare. The amount of energy and work it took to hide my "little secret" made elementary school feel like an out-of-body experience.

It was in the second grade that I now realize I made my first real attempt at expressing my true and real self without exposing the "little secret." It was a magical discovery for me—one that brings me joy and fulfillment to this day. Mrs. Davis, my second grade teacher, announced that we would have a talent show. It was the first of hundreds of instances in my life that music would give me the outlet, platform and freedom to be creative. This is not to say that all gay men are creative and musically gifted, nor that straight men are not. But let's face it—there is a disproportionate correlation between the performing arts and the gay community! Can you say Broadway show tunes?

My first grade teacher, Tony Taylor and I— Christmas 2015

Anyway, it is to Mrs. Davis, and the writers of "Raindrops Keep Falling on My Head," that I owe a great deal of gratitude for creating an environment for this little boy with a "little secret" to live his truth, albeit for just about 10 minutes. From that performance to this day, music, performance and the arts have brought me peace, joy and a celebratory outlet.

Second grade school picture

Unfortunately, the talent show and subsequent musical outlets could not stop the inevitable. Sometime between second and fourth grade, we were playing football in our expansive front yard, and my knee met with my brother's right eye. The damage was severe and required him to have a metal plate surgically placed under his eye. As recently as five years ago, my parents have always suggested that causing my brother's injury on that day was what created so much anxiety in my life. I think I have finally helped them to understand that it had NOTHING to do with the extreme emotional and mental pain and anguish of my youth.

As I entered the fourth grade, my teacher was a beautiful blonde lady named Carol Martinez. Coincidentally, she was married at the time to Tony Martinez, whose father, Don Beningo Martinez, was the next door neighbor and close friend to Grandpa Vela in the 1930s. Tony and Carol have since divorced and remarried, but their sons Andy and Trey remain close friends of mine, as does Tony. Fortunately for the people of south Texas and my home area, , Tony is the current mayor of Brownsville, Texas and works very closely with me on political and economic development matters. It was my good fortune that I was assigned to Mrs. Martinez's classroom, with the family history and all, as fate would have it, it was to be a year of my life that was transformative, disruptive and destructive.

Somehow I made it through the kindergarten anxiety blues and managed to keep them in check from first through third grades for the most part. However, for some reason, in fourth grade they returned, and they returned with a vengeance. In hindsight, I recognize after much deliberation that my severe anxiety was a result of my "little secret."

The secret was becoming more apparent to me during my times of solitude and when I was alone with my thoughts right before I slipped into slumber. My bond with my parents, in particular my mother, was even stronger, and the sense of her protection even deeper. We made several attempts to get me to stay at school each day during my fourth grade year, but the anxiety and manifestations were too severe—inevitably, I would get "sick" and have to come home or just could not make myself get out of the car to face this world where I just didn't fit in.

The result was horribly scary and painful for my parents and even more painful and frightening for a boy of 10 years of age. My parents consulted with our former pediatrician, Dr. George Willeford, who had since moved to Austin, Texas, where he had begun practicing psychiatry. He recommended that I be transported to and hospitalized at Shoal Creek Mental Hospital in Austin, Texas. Once again, the universe showered me with blessings, as my Tia Irma and Tio Robert (my father's older brother) lived and taught school in Austin. When I was granted leave from the hospital, I was fortunate to have "familia" to stay with. For a few weeks, I even tried to attend school near their home, but ultimately I remained at the hospital full-time.

Dr. Willeford, in his poor judgment, convinced my parents that I suffered from anxiety disorder or separation anxiety due to the trauma I had caused my brother in that football accident, and that the therapy or remedy would involve removing me from them and my environment to a hospital some five hours away. Imagine taking a 10-year-old boy from his parents, his home, his siblings, his toys and his home. Little did Dr. Willeford know that the real reason for my pain, anguish and cry for help was not the football accident but a "little secret" that society, my church and my culture would not allow me to share or live. The reality was that the doctor relied on a false premise and a misdiagnosis to take a 10-year-old boy from the only safe place, safe haven and safe environment he knew because he, too, suffered from homophobia.

These days and months at the hospital and on my journey are somewhat of a fog—I am sure that in many ways, I blocked them out because they were so horrifying. However, the few recollections I do have of that experience were the amazing field trips, arts and crafts and the feeling of isolation, loneliness and confusion. I could not comprehend why I had been taken away from my parents, and, above all, why I had to watch people with serious mental illnesses as they received shock treatment. I also recall that to add insult to injury and salt to a wound, my roommate was a very cute teenage guy—it was probably my first crush and not the time, place nor environment for it to occur.

In an effort to heal from all of those painful memories and not resent the people who put me in that situation, I have had to remind myself thousands of times that my parents, Dr. Willeford and many others were doing the best they knew how to do at that time. It's important to recognize the historical and societal time frame. This was the early 1970s—LGBT civil rights were at its infancy, and many still considered homosexuality a mental illness or choice. This was pre-Ellen, pre-Will and Grace, pre-*Modern Family* and a time of great reluctance to understand and embrace anything LGBT. I have to believe that in the minds of those involved, they never even thought that a "little secret" could exist in a typical Texas boy, much less be the root cause of so much pain, anxiety and turmoil.

CHAPTER FOUR

FTER THE PAIN AND ANGUISH OF SEVERAL MONTHS AWAY
from my family and in the confusing environment of the
mental hospital, it was determined that I was "cured" and ready
to return to Harlingen and life as I knew it prior to this terri-
fying excursion. There was no "cure" to be had; rather, those
months away became a stage for me to hone my survival skills,
improve my acting chops and return to pretend I was someone
I was not. I went through fifth and sixth grades with a renewed
energy and having perfected the art of compartmentalization at
an age when most were enjoying jungle gyms and video games.
Call it compartmentalization or just plain survival, I reached
the traumatizing level of junior high. As bad luck (or a premonition) would have it, my junior high was named Gay Junior High.
It was named after a lady named Minnie B. Gay, and the word
"gay" was just becoming the word commonly used to describe
homosexuals—at least in the Valley it was relatively new. I knew
enough to know that the name of my school was a daily reminder of my horrible "little secret." Some levels of anxiety and inner
stress began to gnaw at my soul once again. I went to school each
day wondering if my peers would one day associate the school's

name with my secret. Irrational, I know, but a good example of the anguish one experiences when being gay in south Texas, Catholic, Hispanic, the son of a prominent family and attending GAY Junior High.

It was at Gay Junior High that I began to experiment with finding a way to survive the secret, to keep up the charade of playing sports (although I loved playing sports immensely and I am still an avid sports fan), hunting like good Texas boys do AND becoming the leader that the Vela children were taught to be. Of the many gifts my parents gave us, the commitment to give back, be of service, share our gifts and lead were some of the greatest even at a young age. In hindsight, I'm amazed that I mustered the courage to run for the Gay Junior High Student Council. Clearly, my father and uncles and their political aspirations weighed on my mind, and my political strategy and organizing skills had taken root. My campaign slogan was Vote Vela, He's the Right Fella. I won my first election and became the president of the Gay Junior High Student Council. I share this memory because it was a transformative time for me in my development—I learned that I could lead, survive and even thrive in spite of my "little secret." The living hell of my secret was never far from my thoughts, but my involvement in student organizations was a respite.

STUDENT COUNCIL OFFICERS — Guiding the Gay Junior High School Student Council during the busy Bicentennial Year Activity of 1975-76, have been the officers shown here. From left, Moises Vela Jr., president; Laura Day, secretary; Luanne Stanton, treasurer and Jim Guthrie and Meridith Kuglen, Sgts.-at-arms.

Harlingen newspaper announcing me as President of the Student Council at Gay Junior High School--1975-76

I vividly recall an incident that left an indelible mark on my volatile psyche. Apparently, in a subconscious and subtle manner to be my real self, I unintentionally would carry my books between classes in front of me rather than on my hip, like most boys do. On this fateful day, one of the football players who would bully me and harass me in our male-only health class walked up to me and called me a faggot for carrying my books like a "girl." It was as if time froze at that moment in time as my heart palpitated and my greatest fear of being found out appeared to have come to fruition. It would not be the last time that my former football teammates would bully me.

In these scary years of my life, while finding solace in my school activities and joining the band and choir, the painful experiences of living with my secret outweighed the joys and outlets. It was as if it was yesterday that I recall sitting in my all-male health class. Health class in eighth grade was actually held under our large city stadium named Boggus Stadium. It was a cool, damp and moldy environment and was not typical as a classroom in any way, shape or form, mostly by the demeanor of the teacher and my peers. The class was filled with my former football teammates and many of our junior high football team. There was a typical locker room mentality and behavior patterns that included much talk about girls, sexual innuendo and imagery only horny teenage boys can so brilliantly conjure up. Every day of eighth grade, I dreaded the walk to the stadium for this class. It was an hour each day that reminded me that I didn't fit in, that I was different than the other boys and that one wrong word, answer or mannerism from me could result in irreparable damage to my reputation and future.

My fear became a reality on the day that one of the football coaches who was required to teach our health class participated in the bullying by asking me in front of the entire class of horny boys, "How many holes are on a woman's body, Vela?" Having never seen straight porn nor even wondered about the answer to the question, I froze and so did time. I was traumatized and the embarrassment, victimization and harassment instilled in me a lifelong commitment, passion and advocacy for the disenfranchised, ostracized, disadvantaged and voiceless. Those memories are never far from my heart nor mind—in my case, I was different because I was not the macho Texas boy I was expected to be, but it could be because some kid or adult is too skinny or too fat, wears glasses, is balding, has parents who can't afford to buy them designer clothes, who speaks with an accent, has dark skin or who is different in some other way. As a victim of bullying, I despise those who demean, destroy and diminish—ironically, their hatred and mean-spirited ways are a result of their own insecurities and weakness. No classroom, no playground, no workplace and no place of worship has any room for a bully.

I look back and I realize that from horrible and bad, good can come. In a very cathartic and strange way, I am grateful that the homophobic, insensitive and incorrigible coach and my peers picked me to harass and victimize. Many years later, in me, it created a change agent—one who will remind every child and adult that we are each worthy and that being different in any way at all is what makes each of us special, unique and a gift to the world!

As I entered high school, I inched closer and closer to finding a way to not only survive with my secret but to find some fulfillment and joy. I realized in junior high that music was that platform, so I joined the band and the choir. It was as close as I was going to get to living my true self without divulging my secret. It was a married couple named Alan and Diane Brumley who, frankly, changed my life at a critical stage. Mr. Brumley was our high school band director, and Mrs. Brumley was our assistant high school choir director. They both took a special interest in me and recognized that I had received the gift of playing the saxophone with an above-average ability, but, more importantly, I had a passion and special ability to sing.

In retrospect, I am confident that Mrs. Brumley had an intuition as a creative woman, and in her soul I am sure she knew of my "little secret." She encouraged me, celebrated my talent and instilled in me a sense that I belonged on stage and in life. It was through her guidance that I learned that the stage and performance were my friends, my outlet, my refuge and my opportunity to shine.

Mr. Brumley was equally impactful in my development as a human being. It was in my junior year in high school that I approached Mr. Brumley and acted like I was "asking for a friend" as to whether he thought that if a male buddy of mine tried out for drum major of the band would result in the perception that he was gay. Mr. Brumley's response remains a part of who I am to this day when he said, "Who cares what they think? It's about following your dreams." I tried out, won and was named one of the top drum majors in the U.S. To this day, there are folks in my hometown that fondly recall the amazing shows we put on at the halftime of the football games. In Texas, as everyone knows, football is king, but we made the halftime show something to look forward to with equal anticipation. I made the All-State Choir and won numerous awards and recognition through music. It brought me a glimpse of confidence and self-worth in a journey otherwise filled with inner turmoil.

The turmoil and anxiety of my "little secret" never was far away from my cognizance and consciousness, and hatred, ignorance and bullying reared its ugly head frequently and unexpectedly throughout my high school years. As is typical for many gays in their youth, I was always more comfortable becoming close friends with girls—in my case, Laura Day, Cindy Mann, Sandra Gallagher and so many others. It wasn't that I wanted to be a girl by any stretch of the imagination, even though that would be perfectly okay if I did have gender dysphoria. It was because I knew that the guys would not accept me because I was "different."

Even my father got in on the action of contributing to the disarray and inner turmoil. As I realized that the world of creativity and artful expression were going to be my salvation, I bravely but reticently approached my parents about taking private tap dance classes. I was working as a sacker at a local grocery store and offered to pay for my own classes. My father's response was like a dagger through my heart when, although he approved of my request, he requested that my classes be done in a windowless room so no one in town would know I was taking dance classes. I had to order my tap shoes from Capezio in a non-descript box.

Regardless of the secrecy of my dance classes, the day those shoes arrived was like Christmas in the summertime for me. I took the classes and loved every minute of it, and to this day I smile at that memory. As a man who struggles with his weight today, I fondly recall those shuffle ball changes with a much lighter frame, a heavier heart but the same resiliency and zest for life I possess today. I don't hold any grudges toward my parents for the mental hospital experience, the tap dance secrecy or any other times they may have fallen short. I know in my heart that they have always attempted to do their best and have always had my best interests at the forefront of their hearts and minds. They did the best they could, as did I.

My junior year in high school proved my innermost fears to be accurate. Our high school was open air and, thus, we would have to walk through open hallways between classes. It was a cluster of three or four football players, on any given day, that would wait outside of my classroom each day of my life for about five to six months. They would proceed to call me a "joto" (faggot in Spanish) or a "fag." I was literally stalked and followed by these hateful, insecure and vicious individuals until I found safety within the walls of my next classroom. These insults, innuendos and inflammatory comments haunt me to this day. I wonder how I did not pick the path of so many victims of bullying by taking my own life. I considered it on that and several other instances when I realized that a life of being ostracized and demeaned, a life in violation of what I was taught at Mass on Sunday, a life that was contrary to what society was telling me and others was "supposed" to be was not worth living.

I credit my parents, teachers like the Brumleys, my choir director, Mr. Irby, and several others who gave me the foundation upon which to believe that things would get better. I'm not entirely sure from whence it came, but even in those darkest moments and stages of my life, I knew I was worthy of being loved, and I knew that my parents loved me unconditionally. Most importantly, Vela means candle in Spanish, and somehow I innately knew that, although dimmed by the ignorance of others, my light would forever shine. There had to be a greater flame to come on the journey. (I hesitated to write that line in this book because for all my LGBT friends reading this book, they will inevitably chuckle at the reference to me being "flaming.")

It gives me especially great pleasure to share that, as I will share much more about my tenure as CFO and Senior Advisor to Vice President and Mrs. Gore in subsequent chapters, it was during that experience that I returned home with my partner at the time, Deiv, and landed at the quaint and charming Harlingen airport. One of the many privileges of serving in the White House is receiving personalized luggage tags with the White House symbol. As Deiv and I went to retrieve our luggage, it was too much luggage (we are gay, after all) for us to carry on our own, so we summoned a porter for assistance.

The two porters who came to our aid just happened to be two of the football players who would wait and call me a faggot between classes. As they reached for my bags and saw "The White House—Moe Vela" on them, they looked up at me in awe and amazement—one of them even attempted to give me a hug. It was one of the very, very few times I didn't want a hug from someone! It may possibly be the most gratifying moment of my life when I asked them to place all of the bags in my mom's van and I didn't tip them. I learned much from that experience—karma is a bitch, and justice truly does prevail.

Cindy Mann and I at Harlingen High school prom--1980

CHAPTER FIVE

I T'S OFF TO COLLEGE WE GO. MY SECOND OLDEST SISTER, MARIA
Luisa (Luti) had attended a school in the piney woods of east
Texas called Stephen F. Austin State University. Her example,
coupled with the awesome beauty of the campus and the music/
opera scholarship they were offering me, made my decision to
attend a no-brainer, as they say today. I was assigned to live in a
men's dormitory and assigned a Texas hick roommate from the
panhandle of Texas. It didn't take long for me to realize that the
anxiety of my "little secret" was not going to abruptly end just
because I left Harlingen. My roommate would make sure of that.
He clearly sensed that I was gay, and his homophobia was on
full display in his words and deeds. It made my life miserable,
but my participation in the school of music was providing me
the platform to be the youngest lead in an opera in the school
history and also introducing me to peers who were openly gay
and proud of it. It was my first experience with seeing gay men
who were happy, proud and confident.

At this point, I am sure many are wondering when I dabbled
or experimented with my inner gayness in a physical way with

another man. It was during high school when the drum major of a competing school in a city about 20 miles away from Harlingen caught my eye. He was handsome and sweet, with blond hair and blue eyes, and we had the mutual interest and passion of being drum majors. On several occasions, we would meet at our family home while my parents were travelling or would spend a weekend at the beach and would explore one another's bodies. We did not engage in sex, but it allowed me the satisfaction of fulfilling my naïve desires at the time and set the foundation upon which to evolve and build in my sexual and physical development.

I flourished as a music major (surprise) at Stephen F. Austin, but I always knew in my heart that there was no other university that I wanted to graduate from than the University of Texas in Austin. My Tio Carlos, my father's baby brother, had gone to UT and instilled in us throughout our youth that everything Longhorn was exciting and amazing. It planted a seed, and I knew that one day I would bleed Longhorn orange, as I do to this day.

Unfortunately, before I could ever fulfill that dream, I had to experience another setback and some heartache. My first year at SFA University was awesome, because I started becoming more comfortable, albeit slowly, with my true gay self. I don't mean to be stereotypical, but I was surrounded by many drama and music majors, and those careers and sectors tend to have a disproportionate number of gays among them—in this case, they were a lifesaver. It gave me a safe environment and a judgment-free zone in which to explore, evolve and experiment.

I became extremely involved in the Catholic Student Center, as I would do many times over on my journey as a way to diminish or destroy this "gay demon" that I possessed. Like many gays before me and since my coming out, religion is often used as an escape, as a rouse and as solace. I explored almost every major religion at some point on my journey for these and other reasons.

I grew less interested in my involvement at the Catholic Student Center as I grew more comfortable and secure in my "gayness." I was the youngest student at SFA to have the lead in the opera—in my case, I was Don Giovanni in *Don Giovanni*. In hindsight, it probably was overly abusive to my voice and led to my premature burnout as an opera singer, but it was an amazing experience to sing with a live orchestra and a cast of very talented peers.

I loved singing and performing. I would volunteer to sing every chance I could—nursing homes, charity events, weddings, concerts and, sadly, even funerals. I recall one performance in particular that scarred me forever. One of my beloved music instructors was a Jewish woman named Shirley Watson. She took me in as part of her family and was one of the most talented accompanists I have ever had the privilege of working with. She knew I loved to perform, especially when it might delight large crowds, so she mentioned that a large conference was coming to town and she was looking for a few soloists. The $100 pay was enticing as a college student as well.

I arrived through a back door as I was instructed about 15 minutes prior to my scheduled performance. I waited back stage patiently. The house was dark, and only the stage was lit. It was my turn, so I confidently walked to the crook of the grand piano and bowed my head as good soloists do before they begin. The spotlight was on me, and Shirley began the introduction to one of my favorite show tunes, and I began: "When you walk through a storm, hold your head up high... Walk on, walk on, with hope in your heart... And you'll never walk alone..." It was about halfway through the song that I had a mortifying and horrifying revelation—I was singing for the state paraplegic and quadriplegic conference! I'm not entirely sure how I finished the song, but I just remember running off stage and bawling my eyes out in fear that I had offended hundreds of people with disabilities. To this day, I am meticulous about knowing to whom I am delivering a speech, with whom I meeting and the objectives of each gathering in which I participate.

It was not until my sophomore year at SFA University that things began to unravel. I had not come out to my parents nor my siblings. The burden of this secret in a Hispanic Catholic family that was close-knit had grown to be too much to bear. It was the first week of the semester, and I began to relive anxiety that mirrored those days when my beautiful mother would try and drop me off at elementary school. I felt alone, isolated, lonely and scared to death. Emotionally, I just collapsed. I was paralyzed with fear, anxiety and ambivalence. I had come to the crossroads that so many before me and so many since have experienced. Live your truth—the alternative would certainly lead to my demise. We were raised to believe and practice that the truth was a virtue like no other and that our individual integrity was one of a few things no one could ever take away from us; the lessons and values I had been taught had now come into complete and utter conflict with who I was pretending to be as a human being. Something had to give.

This emotional collapse required me to drop out of college and return home to the only security and safety I knew, the arms and hearts of my parents and family. Once again, my parents resorted to their parental instincts as they obviously felt the profound pain their son was experiencing, and they called their friend in Austin, Texas. You guessed it: Dr. George Willeford. You remember him, the psychiatrist. Unbeknownst to me, their private discussions included a theory that I was just going through a "phase" and I would grow out of it. Dr. Willeford was convinced that therapy from him was the solution. The only great thing that came of this horrible course of events was that I was going to enroll in my beloved University of Texas and live in one of the most amazing cities in the world, Austin, Texas. Little did I know that my life would be changed in so many ways.

I moved to Austin with an underlying excitement that was overshadowed by the turmoil and confusion as a result of my inner struggles. I began my therapy sessions with Dr. Willeford, and each and every time I would leave his office, I was further convinced that it was a waste of time and my parents' money. His line of questioning was always an effort to find a reason to make me believe that being gay was not normal nor heathy and that these desires and proclivity were nothing more than a temporary and irrational state of being. In hindsight, he is one of very few people that I regret ever having on my journey. I am confident that he had no malicious intent nor meant no harm, but I regret that his wrong-headed and short-sighted knowledge, homophobia and lack of awareness adversely impacted me. Once again, I regret that my parents were complicit in this theoretical experiment with my heart, soul and mind, but I hold no grudges against them, for I know in my heart that they were trying their best to save their child.

I remember this next part as if it were yesterday. It was a bright, sunny day in Austin, Texas, and registration was taking place at the Erwin Center, the special events center where the Longhorns play basketball and many concerts are held, among other events. In line behind me was this beautiful brunette named Susan Stone. In her adorable Texas twang, she got to telling me of her childhood in a city outside of Houston. On that day, we struck up a friendship that is enriching and special to this day and that led to some of the happiest days and people on my journey.

In passing, in that initial conversation, Susan asked if I was interested in joining an organization called the Longhorn Singers. They were the official show choir of the university, and it was comprised of individuals who were not usually music majors but from all colleges at the university who loved performance and music. Serendipity, or as my Jewish brothers and sisters would say, a "beshirte" moment. Susan, the line, the move to Austin and the invitation to join Longhorn Singers were all meant to be and fortuitous.

I auditioned shortly thereafter and was accepted, and the next two years were full of Broadway show tunes, thematic show performances, Texas-OU pre-game festivities and the discovery of myself and some of my dearest and closest friends to this day, like Susan, Janet Taborn, Scott Cole, Kevin Jung, Michelle Prejean, Scott DeFife, Ruth Starr, Paul Parkinson and so many others. The vast majority of the men in LHS were straight, and the women were gorgeous and talented, but the gays were present in full force, as is to be expected in a show choir! All of them changed my life and set me on the path to freedom and celebration.

Longhorn Singers at UT—some of the greatest memories of my life

Frankly, it was all of the Longhorn Singers and the entire experience that catapulted me into a new frontier of self-confidence and self-worth. Every semester, my incredible parents would open our home, as they would for all of our friends throughout our lives until this day, and I would bring down 20 to 25 Longhorn Singers to festivities around our homestead pool and a few days on the pristine beaches of our beloved South Padre Island. In those days, a day trip across the border to Matamoros, Mexico was easy, safe and adventurous. Some of my fondest memories of those days were teaching my gringo friends how to haggle with the booth owners at the mercado so they could get a better price on a sombrero, guaraches, maracas or an embroidered Mexican dress.

Those days were not without eye-opening and heart-wrenching developments. In Longhorn Singers, we were asked to perform when one of our friends and members died of pneumonia, and yet another who died of encephalitis or meningitis. What we didn't know was that those were sadly the manifestation of what we would soon learn to be AIDS. Watching our dear friends die among us and knowing they were gay, coupled with the headlines about some mysterious illness plaguing gay men in San Francisco, began yet another round of anxiety and fear just at a time when I was finally getting comfortable with my gay self.

Performing with my fellow Longhorn Singers

My life began to feel good, comfortable and exciting—all of my life, including the gay self. Not only were things awesome with my experiences at LHS, but my father had recommended that I reach out to his friend, Rene Oliveira, the state representative from Brownsville, and inquire about a part-time job at the capitol when I was not attending class.

About this time, my brother, Manny, transferred to the University of Texas as well, and we became roommates. My brother and I shared a room growing up and have always been fortunate to love each other very deeply. We remain close to this day, and our time as roommates during university was instrumental in providing me with that last vestige of family security I needed as I came to grips with my reality. I am forever indebted to my brother for his undying support of me—then and now. For many years, people would often say, "Your brother is so handsome. What happened to you?" and this was a painful continuance and contribution to my insecurities. Many thought that I resented my brother's handsome appearance, charming demeanor and heterosexuality—to the contrary, I could not be more proud of the family man, community leader and brilliant attorney and executive that he has become. I simply love him and my sisters unconditionally and immeasurably. I will never be able to repay all four of them for the graciousness and kindness they expressed to me on that fateful day that every LGBT person must endure—the coming out process. I feared that when they one day would have children, that they would not allow me to be around them or have a relationship with them. Horrible thoughts, but a real fear during the coming out process.

My siblings have been a source of support, comfort and unconditional love too many times to count on my journey of life. The five of us continue the legacy and commitment to education that was taught us by our parents. Between the five of us, we have 10 higher education degrees. My sisters, Patsy and Luti, continue to heal, serve and empower hundreds of people through their counseling and social work. My brother, Manny, is beloved in the Rio Grande Valley and is the CEO of the largest hospital system in South Texas. And our baby sister, Pepper, is changing the lives of dozens of little children in her magnificent kindergarten classroom.

The Vela family grew to have 10 grandchildren (my nieces and nephews), I was often the first one there upon their birth and have enjoyed a deeply rewarding love and pride for all of them, and now their spouses and offspring. My nephews and nieces, at the writing of this book, have also taken on the Vela commitment to education, leadership and service.   David, the oldest, set the standard, as he obtained his dual PhD and Medical degree and is finishing his residency in Psychiatry. He and his beautiful wife, Nisha Nagarkati, also a joint PhD and Medical degree recipient are raising their amazing son, Leiden. Javier follows with his PhD in psychology and his many published articles as a Professor of Psychology at UT-RGV. His wife, Alyssa, also a PhD professor at UT-RGV and their beautiful daughter Alyxia, live in Harlingen. The generation of Vela attorneys continued with my next nephew, Daniel. He and his wonderful wife, Megan, an urban planner, reside in Charlotte with their adorable son, Benjamin.

Finally, the first granddaughter/niece arrived in the indomitable, Marika, who is completing her Master's in Public Health Administration. She is followed by the gracious, Brianna, who has her Master's in Journalism and lives in the Valley with her husband, TV journalist, Derrick Garcia.

Brianna is followed by her brother, , Manny Mac, my god-son,who is a shining example of resilience and fortitude as he lives a fulfilling life with autism/Asperger's and is studying acting. The Vela family was then blessed with a double dose of greatness with the birth of the twins, Alyssa and Bianca. Alyssa is entering her senior year as she is working toward a degree in fashion design and Bianca is completing her studies in Psychology. We round out the next generation of Vela's with Tomas, who is studying economics at the University of Texas and Esteban is a freshman at the University of Texas and is studying business, who just finished being the senior class president at Harlingen High School.

The entire Moises Vela family—2005 at my parents' 50th wedding anniversary celebration

This book would not be complete without reference to my siblings and nephews and nieces who are part of my soul. My heart sings and beams with pride at the mere mention of my nephews, nieces, their spouses and offspring. I watch them grow up in awe—awe of their intelligence, compassion, ambition and commitment to carry on the values, traditions and commitment to service and leadership that has been passed on from generation to generation of Velas.

I was fortunate during my studies at the University of Texas to stop those useless therapy sessions and begin what I call the therapy of love and life. Part of that life therapy was my first real job as an assistant in the office of State Representative Rene Oliveira. The Oliveiras, like the Vela family, go back many years in the Rio Grande Valley and have contributed to the betterment of the lives of many. I had no idea that I was going to be washing Representative Oliveira's car on Guadalupe Boulevard and picking up his laundry on Congress Avenue, but I did all of my tasks with a sense of urgency and importance.

It was that work ethic and those virtues that my parents taught me that resulted in me becoming his legislative director at a very young age in the next session of the legislature. In that role, I oversaw the creation of legislation, engaged in extensive constituent outreach and relations, oversaw the legislative process and gained an in-depth understanding of how state government works. Rene, that job and those experiences were to provide me with the tools, experience and insight to go to make a little bit of American history, as I will describe in forthcoming chapters.

As I mentioned earlier, President Jimmy Carter named my uncle, Filemon Vela, to the federal judiciary in the 5th circuit. My Tio Filo, like my father and uncles, was a mentor and exemplary role model for my brother, cousins and me. Watching him exercise his duties as a jurist, with his integrity, knowledge, compassion and forthrightness, left an indelible mark on me that I carry to this day. Also during this time period, my father decided to challenge a multi-year incumbent and ran to be our Cameron County judge. It was a challenging task and race, but with my mother and my Tia Blanca as his co-campaign managers, we went on to a resounding victory, and Daddy served with distinction for four years. My Tia Blanca, my Tio Filo's wife, would later become the first female mayor of the city of Brownsville, and, of course, my cousin, Filemon Vela, Jr., is currently the U.S. Congressman from that district. I watch him arrive at his office before the break of dawn and be the last to leave. I don't know if I have ever seen a harder working Congressman than my cousin Fil. He and his wife, Rose, a retired appellate court judge in Texas, have dedicated their lives to improving the lives of the people of south Texas. I know Fil's parents are in heaven and beaming with pride, as am I.

Of all the incredible opportunities I have received on my journey thus far, one of the greatest for me personally was the phone call from the University of Texas, LILAS Benson Library of Latin American Studies. The library has bestowed upon on me the invitation to leave all of my White House papers, political memorabilia and Vela family history to the library. The library houses the world's largest collection of Hispanic work by Latino scholars, luminaires and thought leaders. As my blood runs orange for my beloved University of Texas, my papers and legacy will remain there eternally. It is extra poignant and meaningful that my papers and memorabilia will be housed adjacent to those of my beloved Tio Filemon.

During my time at the University of Texas, I will never forget the day as I was driving to lunch with close friends very near the campus with the radio blaring. The radio announcer took a break from the music of the day to update the news. It was then that I heard of how Cameron County Judge Moises Vela had announced that the reason we have a drug problem in America was because the Beatles came to our country. For those who wonder where some of my "outside the box" thinking comes from, you now know! I turned that radio off so quickly and made it clear to my friends that they completely misheard what the radio announcer had said.

In addition to the many joys and life highlights during my time at the University of Texas, I experienced another first during those memorable years. My friends in Longhorn Singers tended to be innocent and inexperienced like me, and several of us realized on one rainy night that we had not smoked marijuana. Yes, I was pretty goody two-shoes, but I have always believed my lack of interest in drugs was rooted in my father and uncle's roles as attorneys and judges. We were raised with an ironclad respect for the law and ethics. I saw first-hand throughout my childhood the ramifications of drug abuse, and I remain disinterested in participating in those destructive forces.

I did have one momentary lapse in my drug-free lifestyle. On that rainy night, I realized that it was something I needed to experience at least once, and I chose to do it with people I trusted and in a safe environment. Frankly, I found the process so tedious and laborious as the seeds were separated on a coffee table before the rolling began. It was obvious then as it still is today—I appreciate instant gratification, and that delay made the experience much less gratifying. When it was finally my turn to take a hit of this joint, I did so with the same confidence as I approach most things in life. There were so many of us imbibing that I think I got two or three hits at the most. I have been told by friends in the medical field that there is probably no such thing as being allergic to marijuana, but I sure felt like I was in the way I was coughing.

My Jewish brothers and sisters are well known for the guilt that seems to be an involuntary cultural tradition, but Catholic Hispanics are not far behind them in this category. That Catholic guilt led me to phone my father the day after my pot escapade to inform him that I had participated in this infraction. My father was silent at the other end of the line. Those who know him know that is not common, so I became quite nervous. After what felt like an hour of silence but what was probably one minute, Dad said, "Son, I wouldn't worry too much about it. The only bad news is that you will now not probably ever be a Supreme Court Justice, but I'm not sure that was probable anyway."

I finished my time at the University of Texas with a legislative session under my belt, a Bachelor of Arts in Government with a minor in music in my hand and a renewed sense of self. I had gained MOEmentum and had some wind behind my sails, so I decided to revisit what I knew would bring me the most fulfillment—Broadway. To this day, many I meet are so interested in my White House tenures and have no idea that at the age of 22, I packed four bags and flew to New York City to make it on Broadway. I studied voice, dance and acting. I lived at the 92nd Street Y where Harry Connick, Jr. was my best friend and accompanist, and where I was a telemarketer to help my parents offset the cost of my dream.

Broadway headshot—how about that curl?

In fact, Harry Connick, Jr. accompanied me on my first Broadway audition as I sang "Jalisco" (a campy and popular Spanish song). I don't need to elaborate on who fared better in our efforts to make it in the industry. I knew I needed to go and try, as I did not want to be writing this book or reminiscing at this stage in life and regret not knowing whether I would have been successful. I have no regrets, but I did experience another life lesson through heartache and setback while living in NYC.

While living in this collaborative and shared environment at the 92nd Street Y, I became very close to a guy down the hall, let's call him Steve. Steve was engaged to be married to a beautiful woman in his home state of Ohio and was studying film directing at NYU. We worked out at the gym every day, palled around NYC on our weekends and hung out as best friends at every chance we could. I did not realize at the time due to my inexperience and ignorance, but I was falling in love with Steve.

Through some relationships that I had made while living in Manhattan, I was invited to an exclusive party and was allowed to bring a guest. Steve, of course, was my guest, and during that evening, unbeknownst to us, someone spiked our drinks with ecstasy. I had not nor have I since consumed illicit drugs, but I quickly became aware that I was in an altered state of mind. Upon returning to the 92nd St Y, Steve and I found ourselves in a precarious situation—disrobed, cuddling and making out. Clearly the results of the drug for both of us, but also a dream come true for me.

As the next morning arrived, Steve realized what had occurred, panicked and said he would never speak to me again.

This was yet another traumatizing moment associated with living my truth. I, in turn, panicked, packed my bags and caught the next plane from LaGuardia airport and could not bear to return to New York City for the next 10 years of my life. I never heard from Steve again, but I learned that love knows no bounds and limitations, and that there are different types of love—love of family, love of friends, romantic love, love of life and love of self. Sometimes the lines are blurred, but I learned a great deal about my heart and self through the pain.

I returned to Texas with a broken heart, once again not entirely sure this "living your truth" business was the right way to go. While I attempted to figure this out, I substitute taught in the Harlingen schools and was reminded every day that teachers are our lifeline. In many cases, I saw young people who spend more time at school than at home, and the impact a teacher can have on a child is immense and powerful. I dedicate a part of this book in gratitude to all of my teachers on my path and to all teachers anywhere. Sometimes people are amazed that I can still name every teacher I had from first grade through my high school graduation. My first grade teacher, Tony Taylor, remains a special part of our lives as of the writing of this book, as do the Brumley's, Mrs. Longhofer and several others.

CHAPTER SIX

I N A RELATIVELY SHORT 23 YEARS, I HAD ALREADY EXPERIENCED more anguish, heartache, anxiety, stress and joys than most people do in double that time. I was finally prepared to engage in the inevitable and that which was expected of me. I entered St. Mary's Law School in San Antonio, Texas, where my father and uncle had attended many years before. I was legacy at the law school, and Dean Raba, who was dean during their law school experiences, was my dean emeritus.

I decided to put aside, or at least postpone, my fervent efforts to "live my truth" and to focus on the task at hand, because I had not yet mastered the ability to do both at the same time. From the beginning, I was not entirely confident nor sure that law school was right for me. I just knew that I would be the sixth in the immediate Vela family to become an attorney, and that was enough incentive for me. The one thing I was relatively confident about was that I never intended to practice law in the traditional sense. I had always been taught that, in life, people can take away your materialistic belongings, your money, even your self-esteem (as I had learned from being bullied), but the one thing no one can ever take away from you is your education.

I participated in several law school extracurricular activities and got as involved as I possibly could without failing my courses. I was fortunate that they allowed me to finish my last semester back where my heart will always be, at the University of Texas School of Law. I graduated from law school and went on to work for State Rep. Rene Oliveira, once again, and State Senator Eddie Bernice Johnson (now Congresswoman Johnson) one more time as I prepared to take the bar exam. I got so enthralled in the legislative session that I stopped my bar exam preparation courses and sat for the exam as a way to get a feel for the type of questions and format that I would experience when I would one day sit in earnest. I did that the following exam date and was fortunate to pass (barely), but they say you call us all the same thing no matter your score. It was one of the highlights of my life for my two uncles, my dad, my brother and my cousin to surround me as I took the attorney's oath.

What an honor to have my Tio Carlos, Tio Filemon, my father, my brother, Manny, my cousin, Filemon and his wife, Rose to swear me in to be an attorney--1992

During my various tenures in the Texas legislature, I had the privilege of meeting some powerful and influential Texas leaders and political figures. As a result of those relationships, my first non-legislative job came as one of three statewide key account managers for a company called GTECH. Texas was a blue state in those days, but right before our eyes was quickly turning red. Prior to that political evolution, the Texas legislature was still held by a Democratic majority, and they had the foresight to pass a lottery bill.

GTECH was awarded the massive contract by the State Lottery Commission to manage and implement the lottery, as they did in many other states and countries around the world. I was quickly welcomed at GTECH, and I dove into my new role with an open heart andmind. And, of course, with the strong work ethic that my parents instilled in us. I traversed the state in my company-issued vehicle with an expense account to support and encourage my corporate clients in their participation of the lottery.

There were many evangelical Christians and Republicans in parts of the Lone Star State who were not at all content with this "heathenistic" form of gambling, but it has brought millions upon millions of dollars to the state coffers and provided me with my first experience in a corporate setting. Corporate America was a different ballgame than the legislative branch of state government and certainly very different than trying to make it on Broadway. It was yet another chance to learn about internal and bureaucratic politics versus elective politics and to better understand that relationships will always be the key, no matter what the job, task or objective.

One of the questions I get asked most frequently by friends, people I meet on planes and trains and audiences when I have the privilege of sharing remarks or participating on panels is, "How does one get to work at the White House?" As I reflect on the answer to that question, I realize that there were many people and circumstances that paved the path for me to serve my nation in that capacity.

What a lot of people don't know is that I sang my first campaign commercial when I was almost 4 years old. I sat on the crook of the grand piano while my mother accompanied me as I sang, "Let's all go vote for LBJ and put him in again" to the melody of the "The Yellow Rose of Texas." Believe it or not, I have a vague recollection of the TV studio, the lights and the experience. It was around the same time that I had discovered my "little secret," so maybe I was already cognizant that performance was something that would bring me joy and a stage upon which to live my truth. The campaign commercial played across the state of Texas as President Johnson ran for his own term as president after completing President Kennedy's term.

There is nothing like planting a political seed early. Throughout our childhoods, my siblings and cousins and I were frequently regaled with stories about how my father and my uncles had run for city council and each of them had lost by 10 or 50 or 100 votes in several attempts. As a kid, you heard those stories, and it felt and seemed like my dad and uncles had run for governor or president! The point of their sharing their stories with us was clearly to instill in us the value and honorable aspect of public service and elective office.

By the time we had reached our teens, my Tio Filo had been elected a district judge in our county. Once again, we watched, listened and learned that giving back to our community and serving the people was expected of us and was simply the right thing to do in life. Throughout our youth, my siblings, cousins and I watched our parents sit on charitable boards, play an instrumental role at our church parishes and consistently play an active role in bettering the lives of those less fortunate. It was not discussed; it was just done.

As I shared earlier, my entire time in Austin, Texas while attending the University of Texas involved employment in the Texas legislature. It was clear that even though my heart and soul were probably more enthralled with music and performance, much of my life's calling would become public service.

It was during that painful semester when I had to leave Stephen F. Austin and return home that politics also played a therapeutic role in my life. When I returned home in such a weak and battered mental state, I felt that my "little secret" and the anxiety that accompanied it had won the battle. I felt defeated, and things seemed horribly hopeless. During the elections of 1982, the statewide Democratic slate of candidates included Mark White for governor, Bill Hobby for lieutenant governor, Jim Mattox for attorney general, Jim Hightower for agriculture commissioner and the lady who impacted my life in politics more than anyone, Ann Richards, who was a Travis County commissioner who was running for state treasurer.

Several of those campaigns hired me as a junior campaign assistant in the Rio Grande Valley, and I dove into my job with every ounce of my being. During such a volatile time in my personal life, the chance to drive the candidates, put up campaign signs, build a rally and even introduce a few of them in front of large crowds became my focus and was an integral reason I survived that tumultuous time in my life. The entire slate of statewide Democratic candidates won their races and, although my role was minimal in the context of a statewide campaign structure it gave me a temporarily enhanced sense of worth. It truly was the beginning of a healing process that would set the foundation for a journey with constantly increasing confidence, an evolving self-esteem and a new and fresh beginning of sorts.

After my stint in NYC and during my law school experience, that silver-haired, witty, charming and indomitable lady named Ann Richards decided it was time to take the helm of the great state of Texas. As luck would have it, my third year of law school coincided with her campaign and election. I begged and pleaded with my dean, Barbara Aldave, at St. Mary's School of Law in San Antonio, to allow me to do my last semester at the University of Texas Law School in Austin so I could volunteer and be a part of Ms. Ann's campaign for governor. Fortunately, Dean Aldave was a friend of Ms. Ann, and she approved my request.

The Velas and Ann Richards

I was back in my beloved Austin and with my beloved Ann Richards. It was through Ann Richards that I met one of the most incredible women I have ever met, in Barbara Jordan. The few moments in time that I had quality time with Ms. Jordan were as if time stood still. With her deep and deliberative voice, you could not help but just listen. And the wisdom and insight that came from her mouth never ceased to amaze me. I was fortunate to meet public servants like her who have changed the course of history and, in many ways, my life.

This book would not be complete without my recollections about Ann Richards. In addition to my parents, I'm not sure there was anyone who influenced and shaped my political mind and proclivities as much as Ann Richards. From that state treasurer's race to her race for governor, being around Ms. Ann, as I affectionately referred to her, made your heart beat faster and your adrenaline pump. She had this way about her. No matter who else was in the room or how long the line awaiting her attention, when Ann Richards shook your hand or gave you a warm hug, you were sure that you were the only person in the room. Her big, blue eyes were entrancing, and you were enveloped by her warmth and that infamous Texas drawl. Until she left this earth, she called me Moe Jr. and only in that drawn-out Texas way that Ann Richards could say it.

I was young, inexperienced and like a sponge when I worked on her first statewide campaign, and she saw me grow into a moderately smarter campaign operative by the time she ran for governor. Thank God I was smart enough to know that if Ms. Ann was going to say something or give you insight on a matter, you best listen.

During that gubernatorial race, she was challenged in the primary by Jim Mattox. Mattox had been the darling of the unions for years, and the union convention to decide on which Democrat to endorse was taking place at old Palmer Auditorium on the river in Austin. Ms. Ann's campaign headquarters was downtown and just north of the river. The entire Richards campaign team was summoned to the auditorium to work the union members on behalf of Ms. Ann. They asked for a volunteer to stay back and watch the headquarters. I volunteered. It was eerily quiet, and I sat there in wonder of the outcome. We knew that if the unions decided to endorse our opponent, Jim Mattox, our effort to make Ann Richards the first female governor of Texas since Ma Ferguson would be much more difficult and maybe impossible.

I sat on this bench near the entrance to the headquarters. Lo and behold, the front door opened and in walked Ann Richards. I said, "Ms. Ann, what are you doing here?" She said, "HI, Moe Jr." and kissed me on the cheek. She then proceeded to sit down next to me. In my heart and mind, she was celebrity mixed with family. I just wanted to know if she had secured the endorsement, and so I asked her if she won. She crossed her legs and in that incomparable, lazy Texas drawl, she said, "We didn't get the endorsement, but we won." I was perplexed, and she saw it as clear as day. She said, "Moe Jr., sometimes you win by keeping your opponent from getting an endorsement." It was one of the most valuable pieces of political wisdom from one of our nation's most talented and incredible public servants.

One of my favorite memories of Ms. Ann was as I was leaving the White House after a very long day of work; she had since become a lobbyist for some very powerful interests. I was walking on the sidewalk on 17th Street and headed to the Farragut West metro when I heard, in that distinguishable voice, "Moe Jr., Moe Jr., I love you!" It was Ann Richards in the back of a cab racing to her next meeting, but never too busy to share that Texas love.

Fishing with the indomitable Ann Richards—my political mentor

To this day, I run into Ms. Ann's daughter, Cecile Richards, in train stations or at events, and it is clear the apple did not fall far from the tree. I tell Cecile each and every time, and I remind her on Facebook every chance I can that I refuse to take Ms. Ann's cell phone number out of my phone. She left this earth in 2006, but her legacy lives on in Hispanic gay men like me who were empowered by her spirit of inclusion, her warmth and grace, by girls and women everywhere whose opportunities are better, higher and more powerful as a result of her leadership and by all human beings, because she taught us the true meaning of equality in her words and actions and taught us that wit, charm, grace and intelligence were all characteristics of a leader. The world misses you, Ms. Ann.

I had no idea that knowing strong, fierce and wise public servants like Ann Richards, Barbara Jordan, Bill Hobby, Rene Oliveira, Eddie Bernice Johnson and countless others was only a preview of what was to come. Public service and elective office continued to weave its way in and through my journey.

Barbara Jordan—I was overwhelmed to be in her presence

In a fateful conversation with one of my fellow key account managers, Camille Burger, she casually shared with me that her best friend, Robin Rorapaugh, had just been named assistant secretary for congressional relations at the U.S. Department of Agriculture in the newly elected Clinton-Gore administration.

Camille introduced me to Robin via email, and I began a dialogue with this charming woman that would change my life forever. As soon as Robin realized that the chairman of the House Agriculture Committee was my uncle, Congressman Kika de la Garza, she took no time in offering me a position on her team. I hope that maybe my skills, legislative experience and law degree might have played a role in landing me the offer, but I have no delusions. I landed in Washington, D.C., much like I did in New York City several years earlier, with few bags and few acquaintances. I arrived just in time for a rare March blizzard and was stuck in a low-cost hotel in northern Virginia. I am forever indebted to my fellow Longhorn Singer, Scott DeFife, for letting me live in his basement for the first month or two of what was to become a long residency.

I eventually settled into the second floor of a beautiful old traditional D.C. row house on Capitol Hill. It could not get more quintessential D.C. than living right off of Independence Avenue! It was a tree-lined street, and the neighborhood restaurants, delis, small grocery stores and country western gay bar became a part of the fabric of my life. The famous blueberry pancakes at Eastern Market were a staple, and my daily commute to work involved walking the same three or four blocks to board the metro at Eastern Market and riding the blue or orange line to the Smithsonian stop which dropped me right at the door to the behemoth U.S. Department of Agriculture.

I served almost two years in Congressional Relations with Robin and a team of incredible people who included Hubert Humphrey's grandson, Buck (or Buckey to me). I served in several capacities throughout my almost four years at USDA, and it was as a senior assistant to the administrator of the Agricultural

Marketing Service where I learned some valuable life lessons. The administrator was a distinguished walnut farmer from California named Lon Hatamiya. He and his wife, Nancy, welcomed me into their lives, and Lon had a way of empowering those around him. As part of my career development, Lon asked me to chair the agency workforce diversity task force. I was charged with meeting frequently with the heads of each of the divisions at AMS, including cotton, fruits and vegetables, dairy, poultry, livestock and seed, tobacco and a couple of others. The heads of these divisions were all career federal employees with decades of experience in service to our nation. It was my first exposure to the inherent and underlying tension that lies in our political appointment system when a new administration takes over. Each new administration has the privilege of naming over 3,000 political appointments in various positions scattered across all the federal agencies, mostly in senior level positions. The theory is that these folks are in place so that the new president's policies and vision can be implemented.

I called my first meeting of the agency task force, and I was greeted by reticence, reservation and a resolve to keep the status quo. One of the most valuable lessons of my journey was learned through this experience. Failure was not an option on my first "big-boy" assignment, so I had to figure out a way to get these folks to buy into our vision and understand the value proposition of making our workforce look like the country we were trying to serve. I realized that the only way they would follow my lead was if they respected me, but, more importantly, they would be hard-pressed not to adhere if they actually liked me.

I began an exercise of heartfelt and genuine connection. I golfed, fished, dined and traveled with each of those directors. I helped them see that being Hispanic or gay or a political appointee did not make me the enemy; rather, I spent hours reminding them what a tremendous gift they were to our nation through their public service. I honored and respected them. I knew they needed to trust and respect me before I was going to get their "buy-in." It was a powerful lesson that would serve me well for years to come.

Over time, each of them became a true friend, colleague and partner in our effort to develop a workforce diversity initiative. It resulted in an increase in women, minorities and people with disabilities that became an integral part of the Agricultural Marketing Service family. The agency was better because of it, and I know the people they serve still benefit from those changes today.

Those years of service at the USDA were meaningful and transformative, but I had gotten the D.C. bug and was starting to yearn for more. On a fateful night during my tenure at the USDA, a fellow political appointee named Paula Thomasson mentioned over drinks that her aunt, Patsy Thomasson, who was a friend of the Clintons from Arkansas and served them as director of the Office of Administration at the White House, was helping Vice President Gore's office look for a "lawyer-type" to come help them for six months. Having a few beers in me by this point, I mustered the courage to inform her that I was a "lawyer-type" and would love to be considered. Arguably, those were the three or four most important beers I have ever drunk in my life!

CHAPTER SEVEN

PAULA WAS SO KIND AND GRACIOUSLY SUBMITTED MY RESUME for consideration. Within a week, I was called to the White House to meet with Vice President Gore's chief of staff, Ron Klain, and a lady named Mary Margaret Overbey, who had been a senior assistant to Vice President Gore since his Senate days. In that interview, they informed me that they were looking for a discreet professional who was willing to stay long hours.

The challenge before them was that the travel and billing files were in disarray—money was owed to vendors in states like Iowa and New Hampshire. Although this was 1995, the vice president and his senior staff were well aware that if he and President Clinton were re-elected in 1996, Gore would inevitably run for president, and owing vendors across the nation for services provided several years before would not fare well for him. I was asked if I could stay after the CFO left each day and perform an informal audit, and then make recommendations on how to make the process more efficient. I went to law school because there was no math or science, but I was not going to let my auditing inexperience keep me from working at the White

House, even if just for six months. Ron Klain offered me the temporary role, and I accepted.

I was given my White House badge, and I thought I had died and gone to heaven. During this "covert" temporary assignment, I was treated very much like a part of the staff and team, which included attending state arrival ceremonies on the south lawn and White House events and socializing with my colleagues. I woke up each morning with an anticipation and excitement I had never experienced in any previous employment situation. The privilege of walking through the doors of the White House complex gave me goose bumps each and every day..

It is important to remember that all the filing system was done in paper form. The office was filled with filing cabinets with invoices, reimbursement forms, copies of checks and thousands of other forms and documents that supported the vice president's travel and office functions. They were not kidding when they said it was in disarray—it was hard to recognize any method or system that was being utilized. I went to work.

Every evening, I would wait until the coast was clear, so to speak, and I would pull out the files in chronological order starting in 1993. I would spread the hundreds of documents and forms on the floor before me and begin the tedious process of evaluating, identifying, assessing, auditing and developing a solution as I went along. To this day, I'm not entirely sure how I was able to formulate a plan to improve the system, but I presented such at the end of my six-month assignment.

The day after I presented my report to Ron Klain, I received a call from him as he summoned me to join him in going to see

Vice President Gore in the West Wing. My heart was beating a mile a minute as we crossed West Executive Drive and entered the West Wing. I had not had the pleasure of meeting the vice president to this point, so I had no idea what to expect as we rode up the elevator to the vice president's office. As we stepped out of the elevator, I could not help but look down the hall and catch a glimpse of the Oval Office and look inside the door to the president's chief of staff's office right next door to the vice president's office. I was truly like a kid in a candy store.

My first briefing on Air Force Two en route to the Valley

I vividly recall waiting in the outer office with Ron while the vice president finished up a call. It was my first encounter with the "keepers of the keys" to the vice president, two beautiful, brightand charming ladies named Heather Marabeti and Wendy New. They are both dear friends to this day. The big, wooden, ornate door opened, and there stood this man I had only seen on television, the man I voted for and the reason I participated in the dreaded phone banking operation back in Texas. In his Tennessee accent, he invited Ron and me in and shook my hand, and we exchanged pleasantries. The vice president has a large desk at the northern end of this spacious office and a sitting area with a couch or two and several chairs with a coffee table in the middle—all set in front of an ornate mantle and fireplace. Vice President Gore invited Ron and me to join him in the sitting area.

I was shaking and was hoping he did not notice. He began by thanking me for the work I had done on the audit. I let him know how grateful I was for the opportunity to be a part of his team for six months, and I shared with him how it would be something I would remember the rest of my journey. It was about that time that he and Ron changed my life forever. He asked if I would consider coming to be a permanent member of this team and be his CFO and his senior advisor on Hispanic Affairs.

I tried with every ounce of my being to keep from getting emotional, but the impact, the meaning, the transformative aspect of what was transpiring was too much, and tears filled my eyes. In what felt like half an hour but was probably all of 10 minutes, all the anxiety-ridden memories of my life thus far came rushing to the forefront, and I knew I was finally going to be okay. The vice president of the United States respected me, accepted me for who I was and made me a part of his team. Words just can't describe the powerful feelings of affirmation, redemption, strength, pride and encouragement that I felt at that moment in time.

The next four-plus years were nothing short of incredible. Unfortunately, no sooner did I get promoted than the journey of life tried to demote me. My partner, Deiv, who had been my partner less than a year, was a naval intelligence specialist assigned to the National Security Agency. I met Deiv on a sunny fall day on the orange line metro train when he disembarked at the same Cheverly stop as I. I made it a point to ride down the escalator in front of him so it made it easier to strike up a conversation. He was handsome and all dressed up in his Navy uniform with his big, blue eyes and, like so many people, I was a sucker for a man in uniform. I struck up a conversation, and it was apparent from the first exchange that he was a man of few words, an introvert and well trained in his guarded ways. Fortunately for me on that beautiful day, I was walking the one mile to my home in this leafy suburb of Washington, D.C., and we had to share a sidewalk for at least one half of that mile. Deiv has and remains a very masculine man and somewhat stoic until you get to know him, so I was not even sure he was gay. I was determined to find out. Things were different in that era—it was pre-Ellen, pre-*Will and Grace* and before much of the equality progress we have made since then in the LGBT community. I'm fortunate that I'm quick on my feet and thought of stating that the fall day reminded of the weather on the previous year's March on Washington, when hundreds of thousands of gays and lesbians filled the National Mall to seek equality. I simply asked him, "Did you attend the March?" I was so excited when he quietly answered, "No, but I would have gone if I had not been overseas."

Deiv—my trusted best friend

In spite of his Naval role at the NSA, and in spite of our profoundly different personalities and upbringings—Deiv, the son of a Southern Baptist preacher and missionary; I, Hispanic and Catholic—we began dating, and he moved in shortly thereafter. There is a commonly shared joke about lesbians—what does a lesbian bring on a second date? A U-haul. Well, Deiv and I were just a couple of lesbians, I guess. We bought a house in Cheverly, MD and built our lives together. As a gay man, I didn't have the luxury of learning about relationships, nor did I have any role models on that front, so I tried to emulate the white picket fence, garden and perfect home that I had seen throughout my life.

In my heart and gut, I knew that since Deiv could not talk to me about his work nor tell me anything about his job, this was creating a very shaky foundation upon which to build, but I chose to take the risk. Our relationship was growing stronger by the week, and that happiness coincided with the new career adventure onwhich I was about to embark at the White House.

On one routine day in the spring of 1996, I rode the orange line to Cheverly metro and began my one-mile walk home. Deiv had already finished his shift at the NSA, so he was awaiting my arrival with our beloved great dane, Justice. When I walked in the door, Deiv looked more pale than normal, and I knew something was wrong. He said I should sit down. We sat at our dining room table, when he informed me that his superiors had called him into an interrogation room at work that day and confronted him about him being gay. It's important to note that a couple of years before this, President Clinton was forced to compromise because of people like Senator Sam Nunn and others on his efforts to allow gays and lesbians to serve openly in the military. They settled on a controversial law called "Don't ask, don't tell."

Under this new law, Deiv was confronted because they claimed to have evidence that he was in a homosexual relationship. Sadly, my FBI background check to become the CFO had begun, and part of that inquisition involved many conversations with our neighbors and asking with whom I resided. In hindsight, it was apparent that he was calling a 202-456 number several times per day, and that was obviously the White House prefix. We knew we were possibly being watched and listened to, and we even took precautions in saying "Hook 'em Horns" rather than "I love you" at the end of our conversations. Regardless, somehow and some way, the witch hunt had resulted in dire consequences. We were both devastated, scared out of our wits, and I decided there was only one solution—and that was for me to resign, effective immediately. I was so new to the vice president's senior staff, and I refused to be so selfish as to put him at risk of an embarrassing story in the *Washington Post*, or anywhere else for that matter.

When I went in to submit my resignation to Ron Klain, Ron thought I should speak with the vice president about the circumstances. I met with the vice president, and I was clearly shaken. It was one of the first instances that I saw an Al Gore that America very rarely got to see, if at all. The vice president of the United States walked out from behind his desk and actually hugged me. He refused to accept my resignation, and he insisted that Deiv be treated with dignity and respect, as he had served our nation for 12 years, and discharging him dishonorably was no way to express our gratitude to the members of our military. The vice president asked his staff to make sure that Deiv was assigned a competent and compassionate member of JAG so that he would receive as fair a shake as possible under this horrendous and hurtful law.

I learned so many life lessons throughout that painful time period and experience. I can't speak on behalf of Vice President Gore, but it appeared to me that he had reservations about the "Don't ask, don't tell" policy It was also one of the most poignant lessons I had witnessed about where the legislative process and politics intersect. The short-sighted beliefs of conservative Southern Democrats aligned with the traditional Republican anti-gay rhetoric and resulted in legislation with "unintended consequences." I'm sure Senator Nunn and certainly President Clinton did not intend for these violating and invasive witch hunts to occur and for some of our nation's bravest military members to be ostracized, demeaned and treated as second-class citizens. Yet another lesson I learned was that I was resilient in the face of dark and evil forces. The survival techniques that I perfected as a young, gay, Catholic Hispanic in south Texas of my youth had prepared me well.

Thanks to Vice President Gore and the fact that ultimately the U.S. military could not prove that we had engaged in sexual relations, Deiv was issued an honorable discharge. Regrettably, he was only granted half of his retirement benefits in the severance, because being gay and obese were viewed as "choices" whereas alcoholism and drug addiction were viewed as involuntary. As an attorney, to this day, I remain in utter shock over how our military code of justice could be so dramatically unfair and different in its treatment of our citizens. There was nothing I learned in law school that could prepare me for that injustice. Finally, with that painful experience behind me, I was able to settle in to my role as CFO and senior advisor on Hispanic Affairs.

The Vice President and Mrs. Gore were an all-American couple, he being the son of a former U.S. Senator and raised among the who's who of American politics. In being around Vice President Gore and interacting with him extensively as part of my role as his CFO and senior advisor, it is fair to say that he was a complicated man in many ways. I'm not sure the pressure and expectations of him were ever far from his heart and mind, and the perception of him as a guarded and rigid man were a result of those expectations. I always sensed that he was genuinely afraid to fail and let people down, and the expectations of him were engrained in his psyche. It made him a very cautious and calculating leader. That said, the Vice President Gore I had the privilege of calling my boss and my friend was NOT entirely the candidate that America saw as a presidential candidate. In so many ways, his public persona was not at all representative of his persona behind closed doors. The man I knew and grew to love and respect was funny, accessible, endearing and connective. There was an intensity about Al Gore, and it could be intimidating at times, but he tended to be more bark and little bite. For the vast majority of time, I found him to be wonderful to be around. As a matter of fact, I grew to truly love and respect the man.

Mrs. Gore, or "Tipper" as she was known by to so many, was a kind and gentle woman and remains so to this day. There was not an ounce of pretentiousness about her. It was always my sense that the only reason she was involved in public life was simply out of support for her husband and his aspirations. I believe to this day that Tipper would have been happier in private life and with the respect for privacy that comes with that choice.

I adore Tipper Gore. She represents what is best of humanity and public service. Proud to call her a friend to this day.

She handled her role as second lady in an exemplary manner and always agreed to perform her duties with a grace and simplicity not often seen in the world of politics. In my frequent interactions with Mrs. Gore, she seemed shy and almost uncomfortable in the public eye. In this sense, she and the vice president were similar in that they were somewhat guarded. Who could blame them while living in a fishbowl and watching in horror as the Clintons were scrutinized and ostracized in an unprecedented manner? From the onset, it was her "realness" and her understated approach to life that made me fall in love with her as a human being. She was always and remains incredibly approachable, and I am proud to call her a friend to this day. I admire her greatly and felt that she would have made an extraordinary first lady.

As I write about the Gores, I will go out of my way to protect their privacy out of the utmost respect I possess for both of them. That said, I can't lie about my observations and don't think it would be disrespectful to say that I was not at all surprised when they announced several years ago that they were separating and that their marriage had collapsed. During my service to them and our nation, I always felt that Tipper had sacrificed so much and given up so much of her sense of self in support of her husband that it would inevitably result in her need to one day have her own identity. I don't want to in any way misrepresent or diminish the love and respect they always displayed for one another. The love and mutual respect was clearly present. It was my sense that Tipper had her own set of wings, and I'm glad that this beautiful and special lady is getting to use them. I'm equally happy for my "compadre," Al Gore, as he hit his stride shortly after the election loss and has maintained his role as a world leader on climate change and global warming, as well as excelling in the investment, finance and entrepreneur world.

When your place of employment is the White House, there isn't a minute of any day that you don't remember what a privilege and honor has been bestowed upon you. Every view is a Kodak moment, every experience belongs in a journal and every occurrence is a part of American history. The freaky part is that you are in the middle of it and never quite understand how or why. I gave up trying to answer "why me" and just started living it with a deep sense of gratitude.

I also made a commitment to myself that since I was chosen to have this privilege that so few of us get, I would share it with as many people as possible as often as possible. So I am proud to say that I conducted between 200 and 250 West Wing tours to friends, family and even a taxi driver or two whose story impacted or inspired me during the ride. I believed, like the Clintons, Gores, Obamas and Bidens, that the White House belonged to the people and that we each had a responsibility to let them enjoy their house. What most people don't realize is that a tour of the West Wing requires being the guest of a staff member with a certain badge. In order for that staff member to bring a group through the West Wing, the tour would be conducted after business hours between 7:00 and 10:00 p.m. or on the weekends, requiring the staff member to do this on their personal time, and many times after a long day of work. Regardless, it was the least I felt we could do.

I remember my first few weeks in the Clinton-Gore White House. As a native Texan and fellow Southerner, I felt right at home from the minute I walked into this historic and amazing environment. It was clearly not the marble fixtures and ornate detailing in the ceilings or the multitudes of museum period pieces that adorn its many rooms, but the Southern hospitality and charm that came from the top down.

The Clintons and Gores set a tone of inclusion and optimism that extended to every aspect of our daily roles in the White House. It was understood in the Clinton-Gore White House that we were in the trenches together, and those times created an indestructible bond for many of us. We didn't realize at the time that we were joining a very exclusive club of Americans who get the chance to work in the White House. It's a bond that exists until today, as many of my former White House colleagues are now corporate titans, mayors, governors or members of congress, or managing foundations, NGOs or non-profits that are changing the world. And, yes, many of them are called back to provide their expertise and strategic genius in Hillary Clinton's Presidential candidacy. I call on them often on behalf of my clients, and I have never failed to receive a call back, a meeting or a warm embrace. There was an aura in the halls of the Clinton White House—one of gratitude and sincerity. As we passed one another in the halls, whether it was the president, first lady, Mack Mclarty, Paul Begala, George Stephanopoulus or anyone else, everyone greeted one another with a warm hello. There was a spirit of camaraderie and a sense that we were given a privilege and an opportunity to make a difference in people's lives. Somehow and for some reason, with the exception of a very few people, every person I met and worked with in that White House demonstrated a humility and grace as if were all from Hope or Carthage. We were in it together, no matter your role.

My role as the CFO and senior advisor was exciting, intriguing and, in hindsight, integral to the operation of the office. I had signature authority to pay all the bills incurred by the office, oversight and management of the budget of the office, management of all financial aspects of Vice President and Mrs. Gore's travel, including advance teams, event costs, logistics, etc. At that time, I worked very closely with the career staff at the White House Office of Administration—several of them are still my friends today and were there when I returned eight years later. As I had learned at the USDA a few years earlier, a political appointee is only as good and strong as their relationship and support from the career establishment workforce. I knew they had to like me and trust me before I could do the job I needed to do for our vice president and his family. I'm proud at how it worked out.

As part of my administrative responsibilities as CFO, I managed the White House Internship Program as it related to the vice president's office. I worked very closely with my counterpart on the president's staff, and we frequently had intern forums, guest lecturers and social events to make their experience that much more rewarding. Although we were never close by any stretch of the imagination, it was through that experience that I met a young lady named Monica Lewinsky. Once I began living my truth as a gay man, I made it no secret and openly shared this fact as a way to connect and gain a person's trust, as I continue to do to this day. Most women will drop their guard the minute they know one of us is gay, because I imagine they know we are not a threat in any way. This was my experience with Monica. For some reason, in our initial conversation, it became apparent I was gay, either by my mannerisms or by me explicitly sharing such; regardless, her reaction to that was to tell me how "hot" she thought "he" was. I, of course, asked who "he" was so I could catch a glimpse of this hunk of a man, only to be completely taken aback when her response was "POTUS." Either my paternalistic instincts or my responsibility as the VP's intern coordinator kicked in, and I immediately told her it was inappropriate to speak of the Principals in that manner, especially the president of the United States. This was right around the time of the now-famous escapade, but it was a clear lesson that you never know whom you will meet on this journey. The rest is history, as they say. In hindsight, I just wish she had heeded my advice.

In addition to the myriad of tasks and responsibilities that were associated with being the CFO and senior advisor to the vice president, our lives were made more complicated and burdensome by the daily barrage of subpoena requests coming from the Hill and special prosecutors. I'm not sure I recall a day where I did not receive some request that we search our files for any document which contained a specific word or name or set of phrases. Keep in mind that these searchable files and documents were not all saved electronically, and on many occasions it required a manual search of each and every one of them. I look back with tremendous frustration over the waste of time and money we spent in these daily searches that were rooted in political maneuvering through Watergate, Travelgate, Vince Foster's death and others that resulted in nothing. Imagine how much more we could have done for the American people if not for the partisan politics of conspiracy and destruction.

One of my fondest memories of my tenure with Vice President Gore was on the day of my first trip on Air Force Two. A couple of months prior, I noticed during our daily senior staff meeting that the vice president was tentatively scheduled to go to the Rio Grande Valley of Texas. Yes, my hometown area. My jaw dropped when I heard them say McAllen and Edinburg. I sheepishly spoke up and said, "That's my home area." It was at that moment that I was indoctrinated about a little-known fact—if the Principal is going to your home area, then you, as senior staff, will be responsible or play a key role in the events and all related activities. My heart skipped several beats. I had just been working there as a permanent senior staff member for less than six months, and now there was a chance I was going to my hometown with the vice president of the United States, AND I was responsible to set up the events and logistics and accompany him.

Sure enough, the scheduled trip to south Texas became final, and I did what life and my upbringing had trained me to do: dive in, learn and make it happen. The Clinton-Gore administration was proud of its policy accomplishment in creating the Empowerment Zone Program which provided additional federal, financial and other support for designated economically disadvantaged areas of the nation through job and skills training and other helpful solutions. Part of the Rio Grande Valley was designated an empowerment zone, so I thought it wise to highlight the success of the program on the visit. The higher education cornerstone of the Rio Grande Valley at the time was Pan American University (today, the University of Texas-RGV). Coincidentally, my father had been chairman of the Board of Regents of this wonderful institution about a decade earlier. It was imperative for the vice president to make a major address on that campus on higher education and housing policies and initiatives. We did a few other, smaller events among the people that I recommended would be helpful in promoting the image of the vice president and the administration as being a friend of the Hispanic community. The trip was weeks in the making, and it was an educational experience for me to see all the details, hard work and effort that went into preparing, developing and implementing a vice presidential trip.

Vice President Gore was so gracious and kind to the Vela family

The day I had dreamed of had finally come upon us. I had four large binders of materials in order to fully brief the vice president before arrival at the McAllen International Airport. The thought of arriving in the Rio Grande Valley—the birthplace of the pioneer Vela family and home to thousands of Vela relatives, on Air Force Two, was beyond my imagination. When a staff member is to accompany a Principal on a trip on AF I or AF II, with the exception of family, the body person, some military aides, or possibly a senior aide or two, the staff assembles at the White House and is shuttled in staff vans to Andrews Air Force Base—the home of the presidential and vice presidential fleet of aircraft. The Principal and their immediate entourage are either taken there in a motorcade or flown in Marine One or Marine Two.

By the time the trip date had arrived, I was running on just sheer adrenaline. I was exhausted from the many late nights and all-nighters it took in preparation for four events—who, what, when and where. As all good gay couples do, my partner at the time, Deiv, who happens to have a pastry chef certification, thought it a good idea to bake about three dozen homemade muffins for me to share with all the passengers on Air Force Two. In order to get to the staff van departure at the White House, I had to leave my home in Cheverly at 5:15 a.m. and catch the first metro subway train into D.C. Picture me boarding the metro train with four large black binders, a backpack with essentials, an over-the-shoulder briefcase AND three dozen muffins.

Somehow I managed to board the train without dropping my precious cargo. I sat down and caught my breath, and the reality of what was about to occur was starting to sink in. It was about three stops later that I realized that I felt a cool breeze as the metro doors would open. The first five stops or so were above ground, so I just chalked it up to a natural breeze from the door opening and closing. Once we went underground, it was painfully clear that the breeze was not because of the wind coming through the doors but because my pants were torn from the bottom of my zipper all the way up the back to my belt loop. It was a blessing that I had a self-imposed rule never to go commando in a business suit!

When I realized the predicament in which I found myself, I also faced the realization that turning back was not an option. If you are not there when the van departs, you are left behind—plain and simple. I was not going to miss this virgin trip on Air Force Two and let all my hard preparation go to waste. My eyes began to well up, but I somehow remembered what my mom had always told us growing up—when the going gets tough, the tough get going! I had about six metro stops to devise a plan, and boy did I devise a plan.

I arrived about 15 minutes early to the White House, at which time I ran to my office and locked the doors behind me. If you have never sat in your office in your underwear, I encourage everyone to do so—it is liberating! As I sat in my underwear, I proceeded to staple my pants with at least 100 staples. In some places, I double stapled to avoid any possible problem later in the day. I'm proud to say that with no sewing experience, I was still smart enough to staple on the inside. I was able to put my pants back on and hop on the staff van. Before leaving my office, I was able to reach my mom and ask her to please go buy me a new suit and bring it to the McAllen airport.

As I boarded the staff van, in my typical self-deprecating style, I decided that the embarrassment and humiliation would feel much less painful if I shared what I was experiencing with my colleagues. I then informed Maria Echaveste, Cynthia Jasso Rotunno, Michael Feldman and several other dear friends that I was sitting on over 100 staples. The laughter and ribbing lasted almost the entire 30-minute drive to Andrews Air Force Base. It seemed to dissipate just in time.

The van pulled onto the tarmac and right up beside this monstrosity of a plane with "The United States of America" on the side of it. The goose bumps on my body were the size of Texas, and I was as giddy as a newborn pony. I walked up the back steps of the plane, as staff does not traditionally enter through the main steps. I walked through the plane, and it was the first time I had seen a conference room and table on a plane! I approached the senior staff seating area, and there it was—a small Air Force Two name card that read "Moe Vela". I sat down and unloaded my huge four binders, put down the muffins and my briefcase and literally held my face in my hands and just took it all in. No sooner did I look up to see my father's cousin and my Tio (many times, we refer to our elder cousins as uncle or aunt in the Latino tradition) Ruben Hinojosa. He had just been elected to be the U.S. Congressman from our home area and, as is customary, the member whose district we are visiting is often invited to accompany the Principal. I embraced him, as is a tradition in our culture, and we both stood in the hallway of Air Force Two and got emotional as we imagined how proud my grandfather and his father had to be in heaven on that morning.

Just as I began to get comfortable with the notion that I was riding on Air Force Two, I felt a hand on my shoulder and I looked up to find that Vice President Gore had come to welcome me onto his plane. I thanked him effusively and somehow mustered up enough courage to tell him how wonderful his events were going to be in my home area. He smiled and proceeded to the back of the plane to visit with the travelling press corps. I came to find out on subsequent trips, that was also a customary tradition for the Principal to engage in "off the record" exchanges in the informal setting of the plane during flight.

About 20 minutes later, I realized that I was inadvertently blocking the path for the vice president to get back to his private cabin, which was outfitted with a desk and couches that made into a bed. As he approached, I excused myself but not before noticing that he was trailed by several of my colleagues and members of the press corps. I had a hunch that something was up. The vice president put his arm around me as all those folks gathered. He proceeded to inform me that he was made aware that I had experienced a "little problem" that morning. He presented me with an Air Force Two sewing kit because he had heard that I might have a special need for it. The laughter lasted what felt like an eternity, but it was my first glimpse at the real Al Gore—a warm and funny prankster.

Vice President Gore presenting me with an AF II sewing kit

As tradition would have it, the senior staff member responsible for the events on a trip is called upon to brief the vice president in his cabin about 30 minutes prior to landing. Those four huge binders were finally put to use. I engaged in the first of what would be many briefings to the vice president of the United States, and I survived. We touched down at McAllen International Airport, and our advance team had so graciously lined up my immediate family members for pictures and an exchange with the vice president. The vice president could not have been more gracious and loving to my parents, siblings and nephews and nieces—jovially exchanging "Moe" stories with them and patiently posing with each of them. The trip was off to a magnificent start, with the exception of one major setback—my mother got so excited that she was going to meet Al Gore that she forgot to bring the new suit!

The event at the university went as planned, as did the walk-about in an impoverished community. It was time for the empowerment zone event, where we were to hear testimonials from locals who had benefitted from the jobs and skills training that resulted from President Clinton's program. I don't recall whether it was the second or third testimonial, but it was a gentle and sweet elderly Hispanic lady with a very heavy accent. Her first remarks to the vice president were, "You are very sexy in real life." The vice president turned all shades of red but was clearly tickled and flattered; the blood left my head, and the lady smiled from ear to ear.

It was this very same wonderful lady who announced to this crowd of 1,000 people that she had learned to be a seamstress because of the Empowerment Zone Program and that she was able to open her own sewing shop. I don't need to tell you where this went from there—the vice president asked me to stand up and announced to the lady that it was her lucky day, as he had a new customer for her! Again, on display was the Al Gore I knew and loved and the one I wish America had gotten to know before the election was stolen from him.

You would think that the end of that first trip on Air Force Two would have been the end of that nightmare suit. When I returned, as crazy as it sounds, I put the suit in the back of the closet for posterity purposes. I'm not sure whether I thought it would one day be famous like Monica Lewinsky's blue dress or what, but there it sat for months on end. Many months later, I had a premature senior moment and wore that suit to work. I pride myself in being alert and sharp, but we all have mind lapses, and mine was a dandy.

I arrived to the magnetometers at the White House, and the Secret Service greeted me by name as they did on most days. Due to my role as CFO, I had to interact with them more than most, on administrative matters, so there was a strong working relationship. I put my belongings on the conveyer belt like any other day and walked through the magnetometers as usual. The only difference this day was that the alarm sounded as it detected something metal or potentially dangerous. I was dumbfounded and went back through two more times and ensured that my pockets were empty. After three attempts and three distinct alarms, we concluded that they needed to wand me as protocol required. I spread my legs and put my arms out as requested, and the wand was silent until it passed my rear end. It sounded again on the way back up as it passed my buttocks. It was at that moment that I realized what was happening. There are many who say that I have a quick wit and, combining that with the sense of humor that my mom taught me, I looked over at the agent and said, "What can I say? Buns of steel." This was 1997—gay humor was not what it is today, but I didn't let that stop me! Ironically, my reference to the buns of steel video had a more personal meaning to me, as the star of that video was my fellow Longhorn Singer at the University of Texas, and close friend to this day, Scott Cole.

During my tenure with the Gores, I took a somewhat titular and de facto role as one of the leaders of the Latino appointees across the government. I didn't quite view myself that way, but I quickly came to realize that due to my access to the Gores and my role at the White House, my colleagues expected me to lead. I adapted to the role as best I could, and part of that implied responsibility included hosting social events at our home. Deiv and I hosted the Latino Appointee holiday party at least twice and several other social events as well. We loved entertaining, so it was natural and comfortable for us to just add these additional 200 to 300 new friends to the invitation lists. On one particular holiday party, we had a "national incident" of sorts.

The secretary of the Army was my friend Louis Caldera and, since he was a Latino appointee, he arrived at our home to attend the holiday fiesta. He entered the front door of our home with his military attaché. The attaché realized that it would be humanly impossible to mingle behind the secretary, as the house was packed with people, and I think he instinctively knew that Secretary Caldera would be safe among his fellow Latino appointees, so he chose to stand inside the front door to avoid the cold of winter.

In a moment of total horror, our great dane, Justice, who weighed about 160 pounds, came running down the stairs from the bedroom where he was supposed to be safely sequestered and decided he either had a crush on the handsome Pentagon guard, decided to "come out" that night or just wanted some love and attention. He did not slow down, nor did he think twice, as the next thing we all saw and heard was Justice's head hitting the body guard's crotch at a velocity that could have affected his child-producing abilities. I don't think Deiv and I had ever sent anyone home from one of our social gatherings before then or since then with more cookies and food as a form of apology. I used my better judgment than to offer an ice pack, although I must admit that I gave it some thought!

One of the most exciting aspects of being the vice president's top Hispanic advisor was the privilege of being a guest at the State Department for the traditional luncheon hosted by the vice president during the time a foreign head of state visited our nation. These lunches were formal state dinners on a diet— with only suits and cocktails dresses, a step down on the food and entertainment and a six out of ten on the glamour scale. But for a chubby, gay Latino from south Texas, this was like a Holly-wood red carpet event to me! I had the privilege of meeting several Latino heads of state and meeting the president of Mexico which was especially meaningful due to my heritage.

As the senior Latino on the vice president's team, I felt it important to exercise the spirit of equality that my parents had instilled in us at every turn. This included my long-standing ability and desire to forge working and personal relationships with people who didn't always agree with me or who shared a different philosophy or perspective. I'm not entirely great at it, because at times my passion can get in the way, but I try very hard to always be open to the value that I can gain from each and every relationship. On that note, I believed it was crucial that Vice President Gore be viewed in the Hispanic community as one who welcomed all of us to the table. This had to include Hispanic Republicans, in my eyes.

In those days, the United States Hispanic Chamber of Commerce, under the leadership of Jose Nino, Massey Villareal and several other incredible Latino leaders, was predominantly led by Hispanic Republicans. Most people thought I had lost my mind, but I knew it was the right thing to do, and my friendship with Jose, Massey and many other Hispanic Republicans to this day is an indication that I put my country and friendships before my party.

I invited Jose, Massey and the then-40-plus presidents of all the Hispanic chambers across the nation to come to the White House to meet with Vice President Gore. We spent a spectacular hour together discussing the issues confronting our community, and I think they all left impressed with the vice president's sincerity and grasp of our issues and grateful to me for building the types of bridges that seem so distant and inconceivable in today's political climate. It was a stark reminder that we have more in common than we do different, and that premise applies regardless of what our differences may be—LGBT, culture, race, heritage, geography, age, weight, skin color or anything else, for that matter.

One of the most powerful lessons I learned in my White House tenures is that the leaders of our nation are human beings, just like the rest of us. They have bad days just like the rest of us, and they take it out on those around them just like we all do. I vividly recall one of those occasions. The Gores' social secretary was my dear friend, Philip Dufour. Philip was the first openly gay and male social secretary for any president or vice president in American history. I am not certain I have ever met a more talented and detail-oriented human being with this uncanny ability to remain calm and composed under the utmost pressure. It didn't matter whether it was a staff holiday party at the Naval Observatory, the stunning mansion that serves as the vice president's official residence on the expansive Naval grounds on Massachusetts Avenue or a small dinner for heads of state or high-profile celebrities and luminaries—Philip Dufour had it under control down to the napkins, china and decor. The Gores trusted him completely.

As the vice president's advisor on Hispanic affairs, I had worked tirelessly to develop an annual Hispanic outreach schedule that would reflect not only the Gores' commitment to and respect for the Latino community but that would enhance his chances to build the relationships in our community that would be building blocks for his inevitable presidential run in 2000. As part of this strategy, I had convinced my colleagues that it was time to host the first black-tie, sit-down gala dinner at the Naval Observatory in honor of the Hispanic Heritage Awards. The Hispanic Heritage Awards were held each year back then at the Kennedy Center, and it honored one Hispanic luminary in such areas as Literature, Arts, Sports and Culture.

The night for this festive event had finally arrived. Under the masterful direction of Philip Dufour, a massive white tent was erected on the grounds of the vice president's residence with tables in the round for the 200 or so guests from around the country. The setting was right out of a fairy tale with the lighting, candles, centerpieces and tablecloths. It was certainly befitting of the guest list which included the honorees/recipients, Hollywood celebrities, television executives, corporate titans and Latino elected officials and community leaders. There was a feeling of an Oscar or Emmy soiree with the bejeweled gowns and designer tuxedos.

Sadly, during the previous night or early that morning, Philip's beloved mother passed away suddenly in Louisiana. As to be expected, Philip had to catch the soonest flight possible to get home to mourn with his family. Needless to say, this threw our entire team into a tailspin. As process and procedure would have it, if an event was happening at the residence, Philip or his deputy were responsible for briefing the Gores on their role, remarks and logistics. When an event was occurring on the road or at the White House, the senior staff member responsible for the event would be the one to brief the Gores in the same manner. In Philip's absence, it was determined that the responsibility of briefing the vice president on the evening's event fell to me. I had briefed the Gores on dozens of occasions in relation to many events around the country, but I had a deep sense of unease and anxietyabout briefing them on a dinner of this magnitude at the residence. My uneasy feelings were a premonition.

I waited nervously until the call finally came from upstairs that the vice president was ready for me to come up to the private residence to brief him. I rushed to the private elevator, and upstairs I went with a makeshift binder that was a combination of my and Philip's notes. Vice President Gore was a disciplined man who found a sense of security in routine. He was visibly unhappy or disgruntled when I entered the family quarters. He was in the final stages of getting dressed, and he asked me to brief him. He requested his acknowledgement cards which were the standard first step in the briefing process. As he reviewed this haphazard combination of my and Philip's cards, he quickly assessed that they were not in alphabetical order. To this day, I believe he was experiencing a combination of human emotions—bothered internally by the death of Philip's mother and exhausted from a long day of meetings and the ongoing demands for him to be "on." As a result of this congruence of emotions, the vice president threw the cards on the floor as he yelled an expletive and pushed my binder abruptly into my chest, causing it to also crash to the floor. My reaction was one of disbelief, horror, sadness, hurt and embarrassment. I dropped to my knees and began to pick up the cards and the contents of my binder as quickly as my trembling hands would allow. All the while, I was looking up and apologizing to the second most powerful man in the world. He took the cards and notes from me upon gathering them off the floor and asked me to leave. It was the longest two-floor elevator ride of my life and an even longer evening. He remained peeved and pouted the entire evening—I experienced my first White House passive aggressive victimization, and it would not be the last.

Everything that could have gone wrong that evening went wrong. There was no champagne glass pre-set on the podium for him to make the toast, and when Celia Cruz asked him to do a conga line at the end of the festive evening on the Kennedy Center stage, I was certain my job security was in serious jeopardy. This was not the "Macarena"!

The entire experience was a lesson in politics that has served me well since. These incredible people who sacrifice so much to serve and lead our nation are just human beings like each of us. They have good days and bad days, insecurities and flaws, wonderful characteristics and beautiful spirits. They put their pants on just like we do—one leg at a time. I never harbored any resentment toward Vice President Gore for that incident, but I also never thought I would have to benefit from the services of our office counselor, Jane, who I had arranged to be paid by the Democratic National Committee. As it was, Jane would meet with my colleagues every Tuesday to hear of their concerns and complaints, then meet with the vice president to enlighten him or have him apologize and/or extend gratitude or praise, depending on what the situation required. I finally had reason to meet with Jane, as I was somewhat traumatized by the incident. I shed some tears and smartly dismissed the need for an apology. The vice president and I went on to have a very meaningful relationship that was built upon mutual trust and respect. I consider him a friend to this day. The last time I had the privilege of seeing him, he referred to me as "compadre" as we exchanged a warm and loving "abrazo" (hug).

It was another ride on Air Force Two that also left an indelible memory in my heart. As part of my Hispanic outreach that particular year, I had included a keynote address to the U.S. Hispanic Chamber of Commerce convention in San Diego. I engaged in the same routine in boarding the staff van, this time without any wardrobe malfunctions.

We boarded Air Force Two only to find out as we traversed this great nation that John Kennedy Jr. was missing over the

Atlantic Ocean near Cape Cod, MA. It was not until we landed that the vice president was informed that he had in fact died in a plane crash. It was shortly thereafter that through our shock and sadness we received even more emotionally disturbing news. On the day that "John John" died, we were aboard the Air Force jet that was actually President Kennedy's Air Force One and that had carried his body back in November 1963. It was a sobering and poignant moment for all of us. You could see the pain and sadness in the vice president's eyes, and all of us were shaken by both the death of what would have been most likely a gifted elected official one day and the historic coincidence of our mode of transportation on that trip.

It never got old to board Air Force Two—goosebumps and history!

On yet another trip, I had my very first and only mini Rosa Parks moment in life, although completely unintentionally, without malice and in no way comparable to the severity and profoundness of Ms Parks' incidentWe boarded Air Force Two en route to San Antonio, Texas for the Texas Democratic Party Convention and additional events. The vice president was to deliver a critical keynote address that would be instrumental to his ability to successfully raise money for his upcoming presidential campaign in deep-pocketed Texas. As the senior Hispanic on the vice president's staff, I often got to work very closely with the president's top Hispanic advisors like Maria Echaveste, Susanna Valdez, Janet Murgia and a woman who has remained a very close friend, Cynthia Jasso Rotunno (or Cindy, as I affectionately call her). All of those ladies remain friends to this day and are in leadership positions both nationally and internationally.

On this trip to Texas, as one of President Clinton's senior political advisors and my fellow Rio Grande Valleyite, it was Cindy who accompanied me to San Antonio. As we boarded Air Force Two, Cindy and I were accustomed to sitting in the senior staff section of the plane with our colleagues. As we walked into the plane, much to our dismay, we were in the very last two seats at the back of the plane. I was not a happy camper, especially since I had the power of the purse which included per diem and reimbursements of the trip director who engaged in this oversight.

I very rarely play the race or sexual orientation card, so that it means something when I do; I was reticent to do it in this instance anyway, because I knew my colleagues would never have done this intentionally. I was livid, hurt and disappointed that we were going to a city that was 70% Hispanic to attend a convention where Hispanic voters play a key role, yet the two senior Hispanics in the delegation were relegated to the back of the plane. Then, and to this day, Cindy has an understated and diplomatic approach to politics, and it has made her a very successful leader and operative. I, on the other hand, have the lethal combination of advocacy with heightened emotion and passion that results from being gay AND Hispanic. Cindy kept begging me to leave good enough alone and bite my tongue, but, although I was convinced that there was no racial or homophobic discrimination occurring in any way, I felt it was important for my colleagues to know that the optics and perception were horrific and that we didn't work through countless nights to be relegated to the back of the plane.. I was not hateful nor rude—rather, I was honest and straightforward. When Cindy and I arrived to our respective hotel rooms on the Riverwalk, there was a bottle of champagne waiting for each of us with a loving and kind note of apology. And our return flight on Air Force Two was up front where we belonged!

It was on this very same trip that I realized that accompanying the Vice President of the United States on a trip on Air Force Two was also a chance to meet so many distinguished luminaries. I was taken aback and in awe that the famed *Time* photographer, Diana Walker, offered to photograph me at the steps of Air Force Two. She was so gracious and had no idea how such a small gesture could mean so much to a chubby, gay, bald guy from south Texas. On this very trip, I got to engage in meaningful conversations and begin friendships with Karen Tumulty, now with the Washington Post, Ron Brownstein, now with the LA Times and enhanced my friendship with Paul Begala, my former class president at the University of Texas.

I grew to love and respect this man immensely.
Our nation was fortunate to experience his leadership.
He should have been President!

Near the end of the second term of the Clinton-Gore White House, I had grown to respect and genuinely love the Gores. I was fiercely loyal to them, and I was proud that I had played a minor role in getting him ready to be our next president. Al Gore was and is a brilliant man. I knew our country would be so fortunate to have him lead us. As we began to ramp up in the office for this inevitable run for the presidency, the political game began.

For a period of time, it was rumored that I would be considered to be the CEO or at least play a senior role at the Los Angeles Democratic Convention. I was elated and would have been the first Hispanic and/or gay to play that role at a convention. As fate would have it, it was not meant to be. It was one of the greatest lessons of my life when I learned that I was blocked by a few of my fellow senior Latino leaders. Regrettably it was the first time, but certainly not the last time, that some of my Latino brothers and sisters would be an obstacle in my advancement.

Vice President Gore and his campaign chairman, former Congressman Tony Coelho, were convinced to select a Hispanic woman from Texas to take the helm at the convention at the request of some of these Hispanic colleagues. I was deeply hurt by their actions—I had been nothing but gracious and kind to all of my colleagues, but I learned that in politics, people will always look out for their own interests, and that the good guy doesn't always finish first. I also learned what it was like to be collateral damage in politics. I am a passionate advocate in political discussions to be cognizant of who will be disenfranchised and left to the side by every action you take and by every word you speak.

I vowed not to let that experience change who I was and how I loved, but I harbored resentment against those fellow Latinos for a long period of time. It was a poignant and special moment in the lobby of the old Watergate Hotel when one of them hugged me and apologized to me several years later. We are good friends today, and I admire and respect him immensely and was impressed with his apology. The others , not so much.

It was shortly thereafter that I submitted my resignation to the chief of staff, as I had decided that it was not worth the long hours and stress if the loyalty I had exhibited was not going to be reciprocated by the vice president's campaign folks. I was disappointed in the vice president for allowing this to occur, but as I have studied and lived American politics, I realized it is a common tension between an elected official's "official" staff and campaign staff that has gone on for decades. Within two days, the vice president called me to ask me to reconsider my resignation. I will never forget what he said to me the rest of my life. In that awesome slight Tennessee twang, he said, "You have been an integral part of helping me get to this point. I need you now to help me go the distance and serve the American people." I cried then, and I just got teary eyed as I shared that.

Al Gore had played such an affirming role in my life as a gay man, as a Hispanic American and as a public servant, but I had made up my mind, and I left the office of the vice president a few weeks later. The farewell party was an incredible experience with over 200 guests and friends that I had made throughout my tenure. It was bittersweet to say the least. The vice president spoke in such loving, grateful and warm terms of my service to him, Tipper and our nation. I, in turn, made sure everyone was aware that the Gores were beautiful and fine people who had sacrificed to make our country a better place. I was and am forever indebted and grateful to the Gores for changing my life, for believing in me so that I could believe in myself, and for celebrating my gayness and my being Hispanic.

*This was my farewell and a great memory of
Gore's warmth and smile*

CHAPTER EIGHT

FTER LEAVING MY TENURE IN THE WHITE HOUSE, I MOVED to Westchester County, New York and became COO of a Latina-centric start-up at the height of the technology boom in New York City. The experience, as occurs on this journey at times, was not as ideal as I had expected, but was another growth opportunity and a chance to learn about myself and the entrepreneurial mindset.

Fortunately, my dear friend, Philip Dufour, came calling and knew that the Gores trusted me and knew of my loyalty to them, so he asked if I would help manage the Lieberman family during the final few months before the 2000 election. As we all know, Vice President Gore had made history in selecting the first Jew to be on a national presidential ticket when he selected the senator from Connecticut, Joe Lieberman, to be his running mate. I did not know much about the Liebermans, but I did recall his eloquent and thought-provoking rebuke of President Clinton during his turmoil as a result of his affair with Monica Lewinsky and the impeachment trials that resulted from that horrific choice. I had quickly lost interest in the tech start-up for a myriad of reasons, and this chance was like drugs for an addict—remember, politics is like a disease, and I was clearly not yet cured.

Philip asked that I come to Los Angeles and be introduced to Senator Lieberman, his wife, Hadassah, the senator's daughters (Rebecca) and Hani, son (Matt), his then wife (April), the senator's two sisters, their families, Hadassah's son (Ethan) and the queen and heart of the Lieberman family, his octogenarian mother (Marcia). I've always strived to live my life open to the opportunities that might be presented, open to new adventures, open to the spirit of the people who cross my journey and open to new horizons. Little did I know that on that fateful day, my life would be impacted in ways I could have never imagined.

Assigned to work alongside me was a woman I had befriended, loved and admired from the past seven years of working in the political trenches, Kelly McMahon. The McMahon Family has gifted our nation with some of the most talented political minds, operatives and strategists. Her brother Tom went on to be chief of staff to Howard Dean when he was the chairman of the DNC. Their brother Steve is a frequent guest on television as a well-respected political strategist. The McMahons are a close-knit Irish Catholic family, and I was thrilled to be working with Kelly once again.

Of all the literally hundreds of political events that I have assisted in organizing or attending, one of my favorite political event stories happened with Kelly by my side. It is pretty common knowledge that gay men tend to be fans of Cher, Bette Midler, Lady Gaga, Madonna and the Grande Dame, Barbra Streisand. When Kelly and I took on the role of supporting the Liebermans at the convention, we had no idea that Ms. Streisand herself would be performing on one evening at the Democratic Convention in Los Angeles. Like a good gay man, I was like a kid in a candy store until we found out that only the family had seats, because it was a big fundraiser with high-dollar donors. Kelly soon was reminded what it was like to work alongside a gay man—It would be a cold day in hell before I would miss seeing Barbra Streisand perform live! To this day, every time I see Kelly we laugh at the fact that we literally sat on a cement step leading up to the stage and used the excuse that at Mrs. Lieberman's age, we might have to take her to the restroom at a moment's notice. It worked, and we were so close that we could touch Ms. Streisand. One less thing on my bucket list!

Kelly and I took on our assignments with the same vigor and enthusiasm as if were assigned to the royal family of Great Britain. We made our way around the Lieberman family suite at the hotel in downtown Los Angeles, and they quickly looked to us for guidance, mentorship and friendship. It was an instant trust, as the Lieberman family is one of the most beautiful group of human beings I have encountered in my years in politics. There is not a pretentious bone in any of their bodies, starting with the senator and going all the way through the family. The Liebermans, much like the Bidens, genuinely live each day with a heartfelt gratitude for the privilege to serve at the highest levels of our nation's government. Being around the Liebermans was refreshing, their humility and love for one another and others was contagious and their simplicity was inspiring. Kelly and I had hit the jackpot.

I quickly became indoctrinated in the traditions, beliefs and ways of the Orthodox Jewish faith and culture. Our first order of business was making sure that the Lieberman family attended the events throughout the convention that would be most strategically helpful to the campaign, and that they were each at the right place at the right time—whether it be the Barbra Streisand performance, the convention family box or the Florida delegation with their immense Jewish representation. It was non-stop. They were great sports and never once rejected, refused nor reconsidered anything that was asked of them. They did everything with the same sincerity, kindness and warmth, no matter who or where. In retrospect, my time around the Liebermans was one of the greatest life and political lessons I could ever experience. I admired Al Gore so much for this selection, not just for picking the first Jew to be on the ticket, which in itself was worthy of praise and adulation, but because he had picked a man who represented the American dream as the offspring of Jewish immigrants. I am not enough of an expert to discuss here the profound atrocity, sadness and hatred that was the Holocaust, but every Jew who has come into my life, including the Liebermans, is a daily example of resilience, perseverance and the power of love.

It was such an honor to accompany Matt and Becca, as we called her, to several TV interviews, delegation events and the actual convention itself. They were professionals at this, since their father had been attorney general and United States Senator from Connecticut for many years, and they grew up in the midst of that experience. The entire family had been greatly exposed to this environment, so they didn't need our coaching as much as think Ithey welcomed our friendship, love and support.

As much as I loved the many hours traveling with and accompanying Hadassah, Matt, Becca and the senator's sisters, it was this special lady named Marcia who changed my life in ways unimaginable. The senator's mother, Marcia, or Baba, as the family and those closest to her called her, was the light of all of their lives, including mine. Baba was the heart and soul of the Lieberman family and I was privileged to be by this woman's side. This matronly, gentle soul of a woman knew no negativity nor malice. I was in awe of her love and graciousness. After several trips to Milwaukee, Florida and other destinations where Baba's presence could inspire Jewish voters and seniors to get out and vote for her beloved Joseph, I finally had the courage to approach her about a couple of personal matters.

The first was the easier one of the two, when I told her that I had grown to love her like my own grandmother and wondered if she could find it in her heart to let me call her Baba. She literally had tears in her eyes, as did I, when she hugged me and said she would be deeply hurt if I did not call her my Baba.

The second sharing experience was not so easy. I had been an openly gay man who had been respected and celebrated by the vice president and second lady of the United States, so the proverbial closet was far away in my rearview mirror. I had fallen in love with this Orthodox Jewish grandmother of almost 90 years old, but I knew that her religious beliefs could very well keep us from growing closer and truly connecting and bonding on a deeply spiritual level. I loved my Baba so much that I had to take the chance of rejection.

I grabbed her hand, as I so often would on our trips, and I said, "Baba, there is something very personal and important I have to tell you." She squeezed my hand and in her trembling high-pitch grandmotherly tone, she said, "My darling Moe (she might have said "Moishe" as she would often call me), I've known you were gay since we met, and I've also loved you since that moment." We both embraced and wept. From that day forward, she did not wish or hope but demanded that the senator consider me "mishpacha" (family), and so it is until this day. In fact, the senator autographed his book to me with that exact message—I was an honorary member of Baba's family, and I accepted that honor with a heart full of love.

During those first several days together in Los Angeles and the rat race of the convention, there was little time to truly get to know one another. We were all under tremendous logistics pressure, and we all delivered. One of my favorite lighter moments of the convention was when the Liebermans were in the private box on the first night of the convention. I had coordinated with my dear friend and fellow Tejano, Felix Sanchez, about bringing Jimmy Smits in to meet the Lieberman family. They were star struck, and it was Baba who whispered to me as he departed, "That is one good-looking young man." I'm not sure she was aware like the other family members that Jimmy was a famous Hollywood celebrity type, but she knew beauty when she saw it.

I welcomed the chance after the convention to go to the Lieberman family home in Stamford, Connecticut. It was there where the senator and his siblings grew up, and it was there that my Baba had spent many years in love with her beloved husband, Henry. I never forget Mr. Lieberman's name, although he was deceased for many years prior to this political experience, because every flight that Baba and I took together, she insisted on us praying the Hebrew travel prayer together, and she would say to me as the plane rose in altitude, "I'm getting closer to my Henry." I didn't have a clue what she was saying when reciting the Hebrew travel prayer, but I just knew that if my Baba was asking for it, it would be done, so I felt safe and comforted.

All said, I pushed my Baba in her wheelchair from the halls of Jewish day schools in Milwaukee to the Jewish senior centers of south Florida and lots of places in between. I worked tirelessly with the senator's handlers that fall to arrange for him to surprise her on her birthday and make a surprise joint appearance at a political rally with hundreds of Jewish seniors. She didn't stop talking about that surprise for weeks to come. I was so happy that we were able to give back to this incredible lady just a little of the joy she had brought so many of us.

I don't think it fair to paint her as a perfect person—nor would Baba want me to. She, like each of us, had some flaws. I'm not sure this would be considered a flaw, but we have all heard of the stereotype and humor about a Jewish grandmother. My Baba was not immune from some of those characteristics, as she would often confide in me about her dislike for some of the dating choices a loved one would make or how someone in the family or around them would act or what they would say. In other words, she kibitzed with the best of them.

In that same vein, I don't want to sound like an angel myself in the relationship with Baba. I confessed this to her while she was still with us, and I feel I need to confess it here as well. You may call it Jewish guilt combined with Catholic guilt—what a lethal combination—but here it goes. On almost every trip we took on a commercial airline, I would be responsible for ensuring that Baba was served a kosher meal, as she faithfully kept kosher.. And, I'm embarrassed to admit, that on more than one occasion, when it came time for the cookie or dessert, I would tell Baba that, regrettably, it was not kosher, because I knew she would inevitably say, "You eat it, Moishe." Needless to say, in the way only Baba could react, when I confessed my actions, she thanked me for helping her keep her sugar count low but did hint as to how it explained the size of my belly as well.

We all know the outcome and the theft that occurred in that 2000 election, and I was with my beloved Baba and the Liebermans in Nashville, Tennessee on that fateful night. Baba and all the Liebermans thought nothing of me being in the family suite at all hours of the day, and they welcomed me into their home in Georgetown with equal hospitality and warmth. They truly made me feel a part of their family, and I am forever indebted to each of them. As we were backstage and watched from several feet away as Vice President Gore called to concede the race to the governor of my home state of Texas, Baba was the consistent picture of humility and grace. She was not one bit bitter as she whispered in my ear, "Some things in life are just not meant to be." I have never forgotten that lesson from Baba—she taught me in that one sentence that you can't argue with fate. Although later that night the vice president would withdraw his concession and the long and drawn-out recount would begin, Baba maintained her same spirit of positive thinking and optimism, regardless of the outcome.

On that dreadful and profoundly sad night in December, once again, thanks to the indomitable Philip Dufour, I was invited to be one of only a couple hundred people to be with the Gores at the Naval Observatory as we understood the finality of the Supreme Court's ruling. Arguably, Vice President Gore gave the best speech of his entire political career in his concession that night, and then came to console all of us who had poured our hearts and souls into not only his campaign but also the many years leading up to this incredible opportunity. I remember as if it was yesterday when it was my turn with the vice president as he came down the row. Whoopi Goldberg happened to be next to me. I had tears streaming down my cheeks, and he literally grabbed both sides of my face with his hands and said, "Moe, don't cry. There are greater things ahead for all of us." He followed those words of consolation with a warm hug. This was the Al Gore that I had gotten to know over five years—the one who would pretend bowl with us on Air Force Two and laugh endlessly with us. The one who I drank Heineken with on the plane and informed that I went to law school because there was no math, and there I was his CFO—the Al Gore who, regrettably, our nation never truly got to know.

In hindsight, it's very easy to be an armchair quarterback, and hindsight is 20/20, as they say, so letting Bill Clinton campaign for us in Little Haiti or other parts of Florida would have probably changed the course of history. To this day, as I'm sure many others do as well, I wonder how our nation would be different today had the man who received the most popular votes would have been given his rightful place as the leader of our country—imagine no Iraq war or possibly the passage of immigration reform or healthcare reform even sooner in time. But as Baba would say, some things are just not meant to be.

After the election debacle, my Baba returned to the family homestead in Stamford, CT, and her health steadily declined. It became difficult to communicate with her in those final months , but her place in my heart and soul were cemented in place. When I was informed of her death by Becca, I literally fell to my knees and sobbed like a child. Frankly, I am having trouble typing this very paragraph as I battle the sorrow and tears once again. I have been so privileged and blessed on my journey to meet thousands of people from all walks of life, all social strata and all levels of influence. I can honestly say Baba affected, impacted and changed my life like no other. As she and I would so often say to one another in our quiet and private moments, only in America can an Orthodox Jewish grandmother and a gay Hispanic chubby guy from south Texas fall in love as human beings. It ranks as one of the saddest days of my life when I rushed to Stamford, CT from Denver, CO to say goodbye to this amazing woman. Proving the sincerity and genuineness of the Lieberman family, as they caught sight of me at the burial site among the thousands of mourners, the senator asked me to come join the family and close friends. I was given the privilege of shoveling three piles of dirt on her coffin as she was laid to rest. I wept then, and I weep now. I think of Baba often, and her wisdom and insight into life has been a guiding light for me on many occasions. I love you, my Baba.

On that December night, I think we were all emotionally shaken, not only because we witnessed the greatest injustice in American political history, but also because our lives were turned upside down. Many of us would have most likely been serving a President Gore and our nation in senior roles in the White House once again, and now we found ourselves unemployed and like a boat without a rudder. Unbeknownst to most, the very next day I scheduled a visit with an older psychiatrist near GW Hospital, and he prescribed Paxil for the severe anxiety that had overcome me. Although I'm not a huge advocate of prescription medication, in this particular case, it was a lifesaver. I came to find out that I actually suffered from a serotonin chemical imbalance, so the Paxil ended up being a two-fer, as they say. I used to be embarrassed and would never share that information with anyone at all, but I am often inspired by the courage of Tipper Gore herself, who worked tirelessly and still does to this day to destigmatize mental health issues. I decided to share that private information in this book because Tipper taught us that by being open and transparent about our mental health, it is the only way we are going to truly affirm the fact that mental health is no different than the health of the rest of our body. I have a sneaking suspicion that I'm not the only one with a serotonin imbalance!

CHAPTER NINE

I TOOK A FEW MONTHS TO GET MY FOOTING ONCE AGAIN, AND I then realized that it was time to "get out of Dodge," as they say in Texas. My former colleague and former deputy to Philip Dufour, Gabrielle Malman, had married and moved to Birmingham, AL. We reconnected, and that led to an opportunity to come work with a marketing and public relations company in which she was affiliated in the heart of the south. My then partner, Deiv, our Great Dane Justice and I packed up all of our belongings, and off to Dixie we went. I was determined that being gay was not going to ever be a hindrance nor obstacle ever again on my journey, and the South was no exception.

Things did not work out well at the little marketing firm, nor the subsequent small business that Gab and I started with a colleague who we thought was a friend. Those months were a time of great life lessons—primarily, going into business with someone is no different than a marriage. And the divorce is just as painful and costly. After all the turmoil in the marketing and PR sector, I landed as Of Counsel at a top law firm in downtown Birmingham. I was to be a rainmaker in the Latino community, as the Hispanic population in Alabama, like the South as a whole, was exploding at the time. It was, in fact, during my time in Birmingham that I became the founding chairman of the Alabama Hispanic Chamber of Commerce. I was often interviewed on local television and radio and became friends with several elected officials on the Democratic side. I learned that my White House credentials were going to be a very positive aspect of my future.

I changed law firms after a period of time and embarked on one of the most rewarding experiences of my life. During our time in Alabama, as I watched the Latino community grow immensely, I also watched in horror as they were treated like second-class citizens in the workplace or realized they didn't know they had legal rights in a personal injury matter or worker's compensation situation. Many of the Latinos moving to the South were what I call "third-wave immigrants" and had arrived in the U.S. in the 10 years prior to that time. At the new law firm, I convinced the partners at the firm to invest in the future of Alabama, and we launched "El Centro Legal Latino." We went about informing and educating Latinos about their legal rights in the workplace and in their daily lives.

It was empowering and enlightening as I drove across Alabama, Georgia, Tennessee, Mississippi and North and South Carolina to meet with our community. I was consistently inspired by their stories of survival against all odds. More than anything, it was an affirmation of what I had witnessed throughout my childhood on the border—people migrate to this country not for their health, not because they necessarily want to, but because they NEED to. It was a privilege to give those injured in the hog processing plants and the "polleras" (chicken farms), respite and guidance. It was important to let our community know that when a loved one was injured or killed in a workplace or traffic accident, there was recourse. I'm especially proud and touched by the fact that I hope we made a difference in the lives of my Latino brothers and sisters when they needed it the most.

Deiv and I became restless in Birmingham, although we met some of the kindest and most wonderful friends during our tenure there. It was eye-opening and mind-boggling at the same time as one would drive across the South at that time and realize that rebel flags were still flown openly and proudly by so many. I have often been heard observing from that experience that "people don't know that they don't know." I remain convinced that those who espouse racism, discrimination, division or hatred are for the most part a product of their environment. Most of them are emulating and simply expressing and displaying what they have been taught. Ignorance is dangerous.

Deiv and I never experienced any homophobic or racist taunts nor insults during our residence in the heart of the South. To the contrary, our downtown loft was a "must-see" for the Literacy Center fundraising and charity events. Among the many lessons I learned in Birmingham, Alabama, one of the most special lessons was an affirmation of what my parents had taught us: You get back what you put out in life.

In other words, I think my experience in the South was meaningful because I loved no differently or any less, and I have never changed who I am at my core just because my environment changes. If someone in Alabama, or anywhere else for that matter, does not choose to love me back, it is their loss, and I don't say that arrogantly. They will never know what my love, support, advocacy, warmth or kindness feels like. I can only do my part on this journey, and that will always be to smile, laugh, strive to bring joy to others, remain a force for positive energy and just love.

CHAPTER TEN

THE RESTLESSNESS IN ALABAMA RESULTED IN A TIMELY CALL from a New York headhunter. Deiv was always so supportive of my career, and he once again joined me as we took a leap of faith as I accepted the role of executive director of the National Association of Hispanic Real Estate Professionals. It required us to pack up once again and drive a U-Haul across the nation to sunny and stunning San Diego. The housing market was at its peak in low-interest, little or no down payment loans, so I took advantage to be a homeowner for a third time and bought a house in a predominantly Latino neighborhood just outside of downtown San Diego on Broadway Street. With our English Mastiff, Tallulah, in the cab of the U-Haul, we made the trek across more than half of the country. Tallulah was a trooper, and so were Deiv and I.

We moved into the house and began to make it our own. Tallulah, I believe to this day, was the happiest among us in San Diego, because Balboa Park, the enormous natural preserve in the heart of San Diego, was only three blocks away and was home to the largest off-leash dog park a dog could ever have imagined.

We spent hours among the scent of the eucalyptus trees as Tallulah romped and played.

I took a leadership role and, as is my nature, became passionately committed to helping this worthy organization move to the next level. It had been started several years before by two Latino real estate professionals, Gary Acosta and Ernie Reyes, and they had devoted tireless efforts to grow it and sustain it. I brought a somewhat different perspective, and I'm not sure it was ever completely embraced. I learned another valuable lesson in life through that experience—not everyone shares my passion as a change agent, and building consensus is not as easy as it seems, especially when it is among my fellow Hispanics. There seems to be a culturally innate tendency among Latinos to feel threatened by the ideas and leadership of other Latinos, but more on that later.

In spite of the fact that I was never completely provided the opportunity to implement all the changes that I believed were necessary, I am proud that under my tenure, the number of chapters across the nation grew exponentially, and that the one national convention that was under my supervision is often referred to until this day as the best one they have ever had.

It should come as no surprise to anyone reading this book, but put a gay man in charge of anything and the creativity factor is going to most likely soar through the roof . I hired a very reputable event company, and under my creative direction, we created a stage that was second to none. The stage was designed as a home (increasing Latino homeownership was the theme of the convention), and all of the guests for each panel, keynote speech or lecture would come out of the doors of the house to approach the podium. Creative and brilliant, if I have to say so myself.

At the end, my differences with some of the leadership of the organization were too profound for me to remain effective and, once again, the universe shone forth on me with mercy and opportunity. Throughout the last few months of my tenure at NAHREP, privately I had been approached by another search firm in New York City that specialized in the real estate industry. There was a very prominent REIT (real estate investment trust) in Denver, CO named United Dominion. An internal evaluation and review of their massive portfolio of over 75,000 apartment homes revealed a disproportionate number of Latinos living on their properties. To this day, UDR is a leader in the industry because of their visionary and intuitive approach to multifamily housing ownership and management. The search was narrowed down to two Hispanics—me and a fellow Tejano. Ironically, I think I clinched the position in a very private interview with the search firm during the NAHREP convention!

As I am often heard saying about myself, I don't have many gifts, but one of my greatest is that of a very strong and powerful intuition. I could see the writing on the wall at NAHREP, but I am proud of my accomplishments while there and even more proud of the fact that I led the effort in conducting one of their best national conventions. It was a lesson taught to me by watching the work ethic of my parents and so many others. You give it your all—you put your heart and soul into the project even when you know you are leaving. I consider this a test of one's character and integrity. I'm also proud to call Gary Acosta, Mary Mancera, Yamila Ayad, Alex Chaporro and Frances Martinez Myers dear friends to this day. Overall, the NAHREP experience was rewarding and I cherish those and so many friendships that resulted from that adventure.

Once again, my devoted and faithful partner at the time, Deiv, followed me to the mile-high city of Denver, CO. We packed up our things, and Tallulah thought we had lost our minds as she rode yet again in the cab of a U-Haul. We stopped in Las Vegas so I could play a little 3-card poker , and then enjoyed the majesty of the Moab area of southern Utah. We knew we had made the right decision when we crossed the border into Colorado and began the trek across I-70 through the majesty of the Rockies. One can't help but feel inspired and motivated when you breath the fresh air of Colorado and you are embraced by the pines and aspens that line the highways and mountain ridges.

We moved into a townhome near the UDR headquarters in an area south of Denver called Highlands Ranch. I quickly realized that Denver and the Rocky Mountains were a slice of what I imagined heaven to be like. Just walking the three quarters of a mile to work in the morning was invigorating. I also quickly learned why native Denverites have what they call the 15-minute rule—it can turn from a clear blue sky with sunshine to a massive snowstorm in a sudden and short 15 minutes. However, it doesn't really matter what the weather is doing in Colorado; the beauty around you is immeasurable. It was not long after we moved there that I thought Deiv might want to get a job, as I felt he was growing bored and his self-worth was starting to be adversely affected.

In that light, while reading the Sunday paper, I saw an ad for the sale of a pet shop in a mountain village about 20 miles up the mountain outside of Denver in a village called Idaho Springs. Idaho Springs is a quiet, sleepy village nestled in the mountains and mostly known in modern times as the home of Beaujeau's Pizza—home to the mountain pizza pie. In earlier times, it was a mining town, as a vibrant and scenic river runs down from the surrounding mountains through the heart of town.

I borrowed from three different banks through lines of credit, and we bought the Happy Tails pet store on quaint Main Street in Idaho Springs. It was not soon after that we moved to a much larger location down a little farther on Main Street. Under Deiv's management, we added doggie day care and a much larger inventory of dog supplies to the already-vibrant pet grooming services. Deiv put his nose to the grindstone and became an accomplished groomer of everything from a standard poodle to English sheep dogs.

I settled in to my role as a senior vice president of Multicultural Initiatives at United Dominion while Deiv and Tallulah would commute each day to and from the pet store. I was managed and supervised by the company's COO, Chris Genry, who is still a dear friend to this day. He empowered me to develop a Hispanic/multicultural initiative to better serve the growing Hispanic population within their portfolio. I traveled to various properties across the country that were owned by UDR, and I spent countless hours with property managers and even Hispanic residents within those properties.

I wanted to fully understand and wrap my arms around the challenge at hand. It did not take me long to develop a fundamental understanding of the multifamily real estate industry and, most importantly, it did not take me long to come to the conclusion that the fundamental problem in service to the Hispanic tenants was a severe lack of understanding of our unique culture, traditions, idiosyncrasies and needs. Thanks to Chris Genry, I was empowered to develop a comprehensive plan on how to improve the services provided.

Fundamentally, the problem was that the vast majority of owners of multifamily properties in the United States were and are Anglos. Yet, the majority of tenants in those properties were and are ethnic minorities. At that time, over 50% or so of Hispanics in the United States rented their abode versus owning a home. The numbers were just as severe in the African American community. What I discovered was that not just UDR was experiencing this relationship gap, but most Anglo owners in the industry were challenged with the same complexity. To this day, the lesson I learned in that situation is a premise upon which I build any effort in business, marketing, public relations or communication: any property or business owner must know and understand their audience, craft a message that will resonate with that audience and have the message be delivered by a messenger and in a manner to which the audience can relate and trust.

I developed what I thought was an effective, innovative and cutting-edge strategic plan that I was confident would ultimately result in an improved bottom line at UDR. Unfortunately—or in hindsight, fortunately—the company never chose to implement or execute my proposed plan. I saw the writing on the wall but had learned so much about the industry and its strained and ineffective relationship with Hispanic renters and tenants across the nation that I knew there was value in what I had developed.

I took a big risk; we moved to Idaho Springs in the mountains and lived in a little old house a few blocks from the pet store. I hung my own shingle as a multifamily real estate consultant with an expertise in multicultural strategies, and the rest is history as they say. I used a small office in the front of the pet store as my office and somehow conducted effective and successful business over the barking of the dogs in daycare. In reflecting on those days, I now realize that the chance to go and love on those dogs and chase them a few minutes or play tug with them was a respite and kept me grounded at a stressful and unpredictable time on my journey. The mountain air and rushing river were quite contributory to my peaceful state of mind, I might add.

I quickly picked up a couple of clients whom I had met throughout the previous years or so, and then I began to be asked to deliver speeches at multifamily conferences across the nation. I did Arizona, New Jersey, Florida on several occasions, Texas and several others. It was at one of the Florida presentations on my expertise of "Cultural Customization" that I was approached by two geniuses in the multifamily industry that would soon become my business partners.

These two fellow Texans, Jim Cauley and Mike Hefley, had many years of senior executive management experience and the financial success to prove it in the multifamily industry. In short, it turned out, they had what I didn't have, which was the access to capital and the in-depth knowledge of the industry. And I had something they did not have—an innovative approach to attracting the Hispanic renter, building their loyalty that resulted in increased retention rates and creating an environment that could result in increased rents and improve the value of the property.

My cultural customization platform had found some believers, and it was a match made in heaven.

These two gentlemen convinced me to join forces with them, and together we created The Comunidades Group. Two of us were actually located in Denver and the other in south Florida, so we chose to put our headquarters in the Denver Tech Center. These two partners were instrumental in educating and indoctrinating me into the world of real estate financing. We traveled to New York City, Dallas and Florida on a quest to raise operating capital and equity capital. Thanks to their brilliance and experience, combined with my passion and well thought-out cultural plan, we were successful on both fronts. These gentlemen were smart enough to use one of the nation's best real estate attorneys, Pam Rothenberg, who is one of my dearest friends over a decade later. Up until then and even since then, I have never seen a more tenacious attorney with an incomparable prowess. We were off to the races.

It was an entrepreneurial and business lesson that will serve me well the rest of my journey, and it certainly serves me well today as a business development consultant. The key to successfully implementing and executing an innovative concept or plan is rooted in RELATIONSHIPS. The entire experience at the real estate company affirmed my strong belief that everything in life is about relationships. . Good, meaningful and productive relationships resulted in the creation of that company, and relationships rooted in trust and mutual respect allowed us to raise the capital necessary. Fundamentally, it has been relationships at the root of all that I have been so fortunate to experience in my personal and business life.

I remain extremely proud that I was able to use my innovative thinking and creative mind to make a difference in an industry that was wed to its long-standing traditions and processes. My cultural customization model was met with much skepticism in the industry—how could this chubby, gay attorney who has never managed a property in his life come in here and tell us that we need to change? Rather than argue, at The Comunidades Group, we just did it.

We bought the first property in a predominantly Hispanic area north of Atlanta off of Jimmy Carter Blvd. The property needed some capital improvement, but it was a perfect platform to implement my plan. My plan involved ensuring that the vast majority of the staff, if not all, was bilingual. All contracts and reading materials had to be bilingual as well. As an attorney, I fully understood that some legal scholars would argue that the official rental agreement that was to be executed was to be in English, but that did not keep me from requiring that a full explanation in Spanish and in layperson's terms must accompany it and be initialed by the renter. I was tired of our folks being asked to sign documents with no idea what they were committing to nor what was required of them. We went about converting the tennis courts to a turf soccer field. We installed additional grills, picnic benches and park-like settings, because Latinos like to gather on the weekends and engage in "pachangas."

The community garden would now grow cilantro, tomatoes and other culturally relevant herbs, spices and vegetables. We converted the basement storage room under the main building into a beautiful community center to host quincineras, baptisms and birthday parties. It was also in there that we taught English classes and resume writing seminars and other such services. And we painted the entire property in colors that we knew to be more welcoming and comforting to the Latino palette. Basically, we knew who our target was, we crafted and developed a message that would resonate with them, we put in place a messenger they could trust and we built an environment that would empower them and bring value to their lives.

Once again, as my Baba taught me, some things are just not meant to be. We will never really know how effective the cultural customization plan works. We began to immediately see the positive impact it had on the Atlanta property, and I remain steadfast in my belief that it would have had the same positive result for owners and tenants across the nation, but the real estate market crashed soon thereafter—but not before my life was once again about to change in profound ways.

CHAPTER ELEVEN

THE PRIVILEGE AND HONOR OF SERVING ONCE IN THE WHITE House would have been sufficient for me and most anyone else. I had become a member of that exclusive club and, frankly, I could die content. As fate and the universe would have it, my service to my nation was not done.

As I am often heard saying, I was "cured" of the disease I call politics after the traumatizing theft of the 2000 election. I vowed I would never get involved again. As noted earlier, I was finally experiencing financial success as a partner in a multifamily real estate company. Although my relationship with Deiv had ended after 13 wonderful years, life was good in the mile-high city. Colorado has a spirit about it—the clean, fresh air, the view of the mountains, the outdoor activities and the wholesome nature of the people all make for a great place to call home. I was happy, and the future looked bright.

Even though I was "cured" of the political bug, I was still very much a political junkie of sorts. From a distance, I was keeping a close eye on this man named Barack Obama and watching my old friends try to compete with the fervor he was creating as they worked on Hillary Clinton's campaign. My heart and loyalty were with Hillary Clinton, since I had met her on several occasions during my time as CFO to the Gores, but I was mesmerized like so many with Senator Obama. Every time that man would speak, I would be inspired, and the Kool-Aid he was serving started to taste very good. It broke my heart when Hillary conceded and delivered one of the greatest political speeches I have ever heard in my life, but we were all to unite and rally around this man who had reminded us all about "hope."

It was one of the first times in my life that I could actually afford to write a check for either the maximum allowed or close to it, and I did so with pride, optimism and excitement. That was the extent of my involvement in the 2008 campaign, and I was just fine with it. Luck was on my side—as history would have it, the Democratic Convention that year was held in Denver. It was in my backyard, and it was a reminder that I was just partially "cured" of the political bug, because I was itching and dying to attend any or all of the convention.

I was so fortunate that my friend Veronica de la Garza, who had served with me in the Clinton White House and who was also from Texas, had a dear friend and protégée named Susana Carbajal who had been named a part of the convention legal team. Veronica and I agreed to volunteer or do whatever was necessary in order to receive the coveted credentials to the attend the convention. I will remember the convention the rest of my life, for it was to be the last public speech delivered by one of my political heroes, Ted Kennedy. For about 20 minutes, I remembered why I had the political bug to begin with—the Lion of the Senate reminded us all what was great about our country and how noble a calling it was to serve in whatever capacity we were allowed.

I spent the fall focused on my business but watching the nightly news and following the exciting election. Not soon after the historic election of Barack Obama and Joe Biden, I received a call from Ron Klain. As you might recall, Ron Klain was the chief of staff during my tenure with Vice President Gore. Ron mentioned that he would be coming to Denver on business and would love to grab a drink or dinner while he was in town. Honestly, I thought nothing of the coincidence that Ron Klain was inviting me to drinks within a week of this historic election—silly me.

Ron has a tremendous, understated and humble style. His demeanor is always one of calm In all of the time working by his side, I don't recall one time that he raised his voice nor lost his composure. I wish I could say the same about myself! I arrived to meet Ron for drinks at a bar in downtown Denver. I had not seen him in several years, so I was a little nervous for some reason. That's not like me, but it might have been a premonition. Ron took several minutes, at my request, to update me on his brilliant wife, Monica Medina, and his three amazing children. We talked about his career and mine, and I brought him up to speed on the success of my real estate business. It was like old times. We picked up right where we left off, just like real friends do.

About 30 minutes into our conversation, Ron nonchalantly informed me that he was giving very serious consideration to being named Vice President-Elect Joe Biden's chief of staff. I was both perplexed and excited at the same time. He was enjoying his career and had reached a stature and level of financial success that most people would not consider relinquishing. But to know Ron Klain is to know a deep devotion to public service and our nation, and I knew that if anyone was going to make the sacrifice it would be Ron Klain. It was not but a few sentences later that he simply and directly asked me if I would consider coming back to serve once again. My initial response and reaction was one of profound emotion and humility. I was so deeply touched that this man I admired so much believed in me and trusted me enough to ask me to serve by his side once again. Frankly, it was unimaginable.

Sadly, the previous year, my 13-year romantic relationship with Deiv had taken its course. We grew apart, as many people do, and it is one of very few regrets in my life. I had to live my truth and be honest with myself, him and the world, so I ended the romantic aspect of our union. I hurt him very deeply, and he didn't deserve that—it breaks my heartto this day to know that I hurt someone whose loyalty to me remains unbreakable and whose belief in me unshakeable. For those reasons and many others, Deiv is still my best friend; he is family to me, and he is my personal assistant in my current business and other endeavors. I learned from that experience that when romance is over, one should strive to remain in one another's lives in a positive and impactful manner. There is no reason to be enemies nor a negative influence onone another. The memories I created with Deiv as we traveled the world, hosted dozens of dinner parties, planted many a flower, raised several canine children and were business partners and life partners are memories that I cherish. He will always have a special place in my heart.

Most people would think I had lost my mind, but with tears in my eyes and with a heart full of gratitude, I informed Ron Klain that I did not feel it was appropriate to leave my business and my partners at the crucial time in our business' development. We had just raised several millions of dollars from an equity partner, and I felt I owed it to them and my business concept to see it through to fruition. Ron, in his typical reassuring and supportive way, encouraged me to sleep on it.

I don't recall whether it was him or Vice President-Elect Biden who called me a few days later and used the phrase "your country needs you," at which time I could resist no longer and simply asked, "When do I start?" My deep convictions and calling to serve, my profound love for my country, the opportunity to make a small piece of American history and the hope and change the Obama-Biden ticket promised, turned out to be too powerful to resist. I discussed it with my business partners, called Pam Rothenberg to begin the divestment process, began the FBI background check the next week and found a realtor who began the search for a rental house that would house three Great Danes and one English Mastiff—not an easy task! And yes, even Deiv came along in a new and different role.

Immediately, it was apparent that I had made the right choice. Here I was living in the mile-high city of Denver, and I was summoned to the FBI Denver office to begin my interviews and background check. For those who have not experienced this process, even when you know that you have nothing to hide, this process instills a slight feeling of anxiety mixed with fear and a definite sentiment of invasion of privacy. The questions they ask leave no stone unturned, and they involve every place you have lived, your neighbors, friends, co-workers and family, as well as every place you have worked. You even have to document every trip outside the United States you have taken! Although I had experienced this process before, it was still daunting, invasive and scary.

As I arrived at the Denver FBI office, the agents tended to be emotionless due to their roles and you got this very real sense that they held their cards very close to their vests. Anyone who knows me knows this is not an environment that is conducive to my personality. I tend to enter any office, room or event with a smile and a desire to converse with anyone who is willing to listen. I tried every Moe Vela trick in the book, but I could not muster a smile nor a laugh, and I knew this was going to be a very long several hours. It did not help that Ron Klain, on behalf of the Vice President-Elect , had requested an "expedited" background check, which meant they had to put more people on the investigation team and work twice as fast and hard to finish the process sooner.

The reason I said that it was apparent the universe had this in store for me was because the FBI agent assigned to my case entered the room. As he read the name on my file to begin the inquisition, he calmly asked me if I was related to U.S. District Judge Filemon Vela from the Rio Grande Valley of Texas. A rush of relief came over my body as I answered in the affirmative, advising him that he was my tio (uncle). The agent's face now displayed the first smile and a sense of warmth I had yet to experience in that office as he informed me that he was assigned to protect my uncle for several years earlier in his career.

The first 15 minutes of my FBI background check were spent in an exchange of heartfelt and emotional remembrances of a man I admired, loved and respected very deeply—it turns out, the FBI agent shared all of those sentiments about my Tio Filo. In a very strange way, I felt my uncle was with me on that day, and that exchange invoked in me the strength and courage I was taught and that I receive from being a Vela. The interview was a piece of cake from that moment on, in spite of the fact that they discovered I owed Sprint around $50 or so and Saks 5th Avenue around $240 from possibly my college days! I paid them and moved on.

Without a doubt, one of the highlights of the FBI background check occurred a few weeks after the interview, during the time period where agents in different regions of the country began interviewing persons of interest from my past to corroborate what I shared in my interview. I have learned during this entire experience that the FBI and any administration will and often do overlook minor incidences such as traffic tickets, temporary credit issues and even the one marijuana joint I smoked while at the University of Texas, but anything much more serious than that is unacceptable. The initial interview sets the stage, and their interviews with the people you have lived with, worked with and associate with are the key as they proceed to corroborate the facts. You just can't lie—better to tell them everything, because if they find it out from someone other than you, that is when the situation becomes critical.

I digress. Back to one of my favorite memories of the background check. As part of the extensive investigation, you are asked to provide the names and contact information of three people who have known you most of your life and who can attest to your character, integrity and honesty. We are so blessed to have been brought up with a circle of family friends that we loved like family. The pool of people to pick from for this short list was very difficult, as I knew that, in typical Latino tradition, the family friends I did not name on the list were going to be "sentidos" (get their feelings hurt). This added more pressure to me in my decision. In the end, one of the three people I chose was a woman named Edna Tamayo, who had known me since I was a little kid. The Tamayos are a prominent family in Harlingen—the Vela kids and the Tamayo kids grew up like family. I admire and love Mrs. T, as we call her, and I knew that she would be an excellent reference. I also knew that the FBI would thoroughly enjoy the experience of interviewing Edna Tamayo—she is articulate, fiercely loyal, funny and gracious.

In the Hispanic culture, as in many other cultures, who your parents choose as your godparents for communion and confirmation are a big deal. This is your padrino (godfather) and your madrina (godmother). Parents traditionally choose someone close to them who they are confident will be an excellent role model for the godchild. In my case, my parents chose exceptionally well in Ruben and Dolores Rodriguez. For my second choice, I went with my madrina, Dolores Rodriguez. She literally had known me since birth. I was confident that she could speak as to my character with great detail.

It was my beloved godmother who provided me and others with one of my favorite FBI stories of all time! First, when the FBI agent made the appointment to come to her home to interview her, she had found out that Mrs. T had hosted the agent at the local IHOP for breakfast. My madrina was not to be outdone. This is a prime example of our Latino culture—although

Mrs. T and my madrina are close and lifelong friends, we Hispanics tend to view everything as a little competition, and my godmother was not to be beat when it came to hospitality for the FBI agent!

I am told that my madrina welcomed the FBI agent into her home, and since it was the week before Christmas, she had a spread for 50 guests of homemade cookies and tamales. I am going to out on a limb and say that I bet there has never been nor will there ever be another FBI agent who got Christmas cookies and tamales during an investigatory interview!

That's not even my favorite part. Before I share that story, I must describe my godmother a little more. She is a humble, put-together, smart, fiercely loyal and lovingly warm woman. She exudes grace and love. She is a traditional Hispanic woman of that generationand was an educator for over 30 years. As is the case with many folks in our Hispanic community and in the Valley, she had a traditional and slight Latino accent and often broke into Spanglish.

Like my mother and several other educated Hispanics of that generation, there are words in English that they might not understand the first time around. It was relayed to me after the conclusion of my background check, of course, that as the agent was questioning my godmother, one of the questions asked was, "Does Mr. Vela support terrorism?" To the dismay of the agent, my madrina responded, "Of course Moey (as she affectionately calls me) does." Thankfully the agent tried again: "Mrs. Rodriguez, does Mr. Vela support terrorism?" My madrina then said, "Moey has always supported tourism." An international incident was avoided, and my background check proved to be successful. Being bilingual and from the Valley is powerful, but this is where knowing more than one language gets dangerous!

Ron Klain asked me to start in mid-December, and I told him that I loved him and the Bidens but that it was impossible, as I had to wind down my involvement in my company, pack the house, find a place to live in the D.C. area and go on a New Year's cruise with my family. Ron reluctantly conceded, and I became a part of the transition team the first week of January 2009.

On my very first day at the transition office, I got my badge and went up the elevator to the vice president's area. I no sooner turned the wrong direction than I ran into Brad Kiley, with whom I had served before, and Cameron Moody. Brad was hoping to be and ultimately became the assistant to the president for Management and Administration, and Cameron, the director of the Office of Administration. As I hugged them and felt that sense of old home week, I made my way toward the Biden area, but not before I ran into another familiar face. Unbelievably and unbeknownst to me, Kelly McMahon, of Streisand and Lieberman history, was on the transition team.

We hugged and reminisced, and she offered to give me a tour. Ironically, on that little tour, Kelly was showing me the various areas of the vast space where the different subject matter and agency experts were housed, as well as the president elect's political, operational and administrative folks. As we walked the halls freely on my first day, Kelly introduced me to people I had not met, since I was not involved on the campaign. In entering one of those rooms on that little tour, both Kelly and I were completely shocked when we realized that we had just come upon a man named Barack Obama as he was getting a haircut and make-up applied in preparation for one of his many press events.

We froze in the doorway, and the man I had voted for and who inspired me and was a big reason I gave up my company and a comfortable life in Denver for was sitting right before me. With that big and warm smile of his, he said, "Don't be shy, come on in." Kelly and I appeared as if we were tiptoeing, I'm sure, with the apprehension of little children entering the dentist's office. He shook our hands and asked what role we were playing in the transition. I informed him that it was my first day and that I would be Vice President Biden's director of Management and Administration. He welcomed me and thanked me for my service. It was a thrill to meet him, and I found it ironic that I had met Barack Obama before I met my new boss, Joe Biden.

I got settled in to my transition role and went to the White House, as is customary during transition to meet with the current person who has your role. Vice President Cheney's deputy chief of staff for Management and Administration was warm and welcoming to me. She offered to help me in any way she could and updated me on changes that had occurred since I was last in this role. We spent a few hours together, and it was a few hours of mixed emotions for me on a personal level. It was this euphoric feeling to be back in this magical place again, and it brought back so many incredible memories.

It was also an exciting and anticipatory time, as we were just a couple of weeks from the inauguration of a new president and vice president. I also felt sad and angry—sad because I could not escape the feeling that Cheney and his staff should never have even been there, and angry because I was reminded of the injustice of that election. I even remember feeling disgust at moments as I visited with this kind lady, not necessarily at her, because she was gracious, but at what her boss had done to our country. I've never been a fan of Dick Cheney—I find him cold, callous, calculating and conniving. There are other "C" words I would like to use, but I want my book to be allowed in schools!

As we worked feverishly and crammed two and three colleagues into offices at the transition office, I met with my new senior staff colleagues and met with various White House officials in the budget, administrative, operations and military offices. Many of the Biden team respected my previous service and would humbly look to me for guidance and insight. It made me feel proud, utilized and valued.

It also created a bond between me and Cynthia Hogan, the General Counsel; Cathy Russell, Dr. Biden's chief of staff and currently an ambassador at the State Department; Tony Blinken, the national security advisor, and currently the Deputy Secretary of State; Terrell McSweeney, the Domestic Policy director and currently a commissioner at the Federal Trade Commission; Pete Selridge, our director of advance and now the Chief of Protocol at the State Department, Jay Carney, our communications director who went on to become President Obama's press secretary; and Evan Ryan, our director of Public Engagement, who is also currently an Assistant Secretary of State at the State Department.

I came back this second time much more mature and confident, with a deep sense of belonging. I conscientiously decided that if I was going to take a 72% cut in pay—yes, a 72% cut in pay—and lose my interest in my company, that I was going to be nobody else but me, enjoy every minute of the experience, laugh as often as possible and develop new relationships that I knew will be meaningful the rest of my journey. It did not take me long to inject my brand of humor. At the very first senior staff meeting at the transition office, Ron, our fearless leader, had us all around a table: Tony, Terrell, Cathy, Cynthia, Evan, Jay and several others. As we went around the table, in so many ways, I was odd man out, since I had not worked for Senator Biden on the Hill like so many of them. I knew that I was going to have to earn their trust and respect. I believed then and I believe now that humor is the greatest tool and my tool of choice to build connection, chemistry and compatibility. There is no bond like humor, if you take one second to realize, when you laugh with another human being, it doesn't matter if it is your enemy, at that moment in time you actually like one another.

When it came my turn, much to my horror and dismay, I looked and realized that I had literally put on one shoe of one type and another shoe of another. I was living out of a suitcase at the time. As it was my turn to speak, I lifted my feet above the desk and said, "Hi, I'm Moe Vela, and it's nice to meet you. I want you to know that today I'm experiencing every gay man's worst nightmare—I have two different shoes on." I am good friends with almost every person in that room to this day. It was a life lesson that I implement as often as possible. There are a few fundamental and basic things that bond all of humanity—no matter our socio-economic status, sexual or gender orientation, heritage, age, race, creed, gender or geographic origin. Those few bonding traits are love, laughter and the fact that we all suffer from insecurities—thus we are all vulnerable. By sharing my shoe experience, I exposed my vulnerability through humor, much like I did with my stapled suit pants. From that moment on, we were all equal—equally excited, equally scared and equally honored for the privilege to serve.

It was not until several days after I started at transition that I finally got to meet this man whose career I had admired since my days in the Clinton-Gore White House, this senator from little Delaware whose story always moved me. It was an awkward first meeting, because the Vice President-Elect was late to meet me. He finished his meeting in one room as I awaited him in the room next door. It was strange that I felt more excited than nervous and more confident than worried. Having lived and experienced this before provided me with a foundation of humble confidence mixed with pride that this time I knew I belonged and was worthy.

As the Vice President-Elect approached the door, I soon realized that he was late because he was meeting with none other than Bill Gates. Imagine meeting Joe Biden and Bill Gates at the same time for the first time! The vice president and I were afforded some private time and then and there began an abiding relationship I cherish and value. As he hugged me when we met, I knew that this man was my kind of human being. He didn't disappoint.

I simply adore Vice President Biden—genuine, real, warm, kind.

One of my favorite memories of transition was on Inauguration Day. It is so easy to just see the pomp and circumstance on the television, and it all seems like a fairy tale. But behind the scenes there are numerous and complicated processes occurring. Have you ever wondered, like I have, how the transfer of power actually occurs? The president, according to law, is to be sworn in at high noon. *When do the Cheney people leave and the Biden people begin?* I wondered. *Does that Cheney staffer sit at her desk until I arrive?* This part was new to me, as I became a Gore staffer at the end of the first Clinton term.

CHAPTER TWELVE

AS TRADITION WOULD HAVE IT, CYNTHIA HOGAN, OUR GENERAL counsel and I, were not allowed to go the actual inauguration on the capitol steps. Rather we met and watched at the famous Mayflower Hotel lobby on a big-screen TV with dozens of others. I looked around the room at the look in people's eyes, filled with anticipation of hope, change and pride in the history that was taking place before our eyes. Cynthia and me would whisper to one another and giggle as we said, "If they only knew what we are about to go do."

At about 11:45 a.m. and waiting until the last second possible, Cynthia and me scurried the several blocks to the White House down Connecticut then 17th Street. We were instructed to be at the Southwest Gate on West Executive Drive at noon. We ran up to the gate just on time. The keys to the vice president's suite of offices were handed to Cynthia and me. We were cleared through Secret Service to enter the compound, and with a ring full of keys, I walked Cynthia to her office and then walked into mine, which was strategically adjacent to hers. I just sat there quietly and took it all in. It was historic to me personally, as I had just proven that a gay and Hispanic man can serve not once but twice in the White House in a senior role, though it was clearly much more important, impactful and historic to our nation that we had elected the first African American president in our nation's history. I was truly overcome with pride and emotion as those realities sunk in.

For a few minutes before my responsibilities would rudely awaken me, I thought of my parents, my siblings, my grandparents, my nephews and nieces, my teachers and the many friends who had sustained me, loved me, believed in me and supported me so that I could sit in that massive office in that high-back chair with massive responsibilities once again. I also reflected on how unimportant I was in the big scheme of life but how I hoped that by serving my country again and making American history, that some gay, lesbian, transgendered or Hispanic somewhere would know we had knocked down one more barrier, opened another door and created another opportunity for both communities.

I did not have the luxury of reflecting too long, as I held the keys to all the offices and also had to make sure the vice president's West Wing office was open for business. To my dismay, I discovered after attempting to open the offices on our floor of the executive office building that the keys I was given did not seem to open most of the locks. I called the Secret Service to help me figure out what was wrong. I was hoping it was not my inability to work the keys and the locks. We discovered together that many of the locks seemed to have been changed to one master key of sorts. Some of the offices had security pads with codes beside the door, but those had to be reset in subsequent days. I was left to wonder why someone would have changed most of the locks to be opened by one master key. My first stressful order of business was to identify a locksmith on Inauguration Day and get them into the building to begin the tedious process of rekeying the majority of the doors to my colleagues' offices. With a just few minutes to spare the next morning, my colleagues were able to enter their assigned offices, and the requests and realities of working in the White House began for most of them. As a point of interest only because I am confident they have been reassigned, I can share that I used my birthday as the number code for all the doors so that my colleagues could never forget my birthday!

Without the experience of having done much of this job before and knowing the ins and outs of managing the vice president's office, I would have been lost and overwhelmed, but I'm proud to say that my Jewish angel, Ron Klain, knew he could count on me and looked to me to bring some sense of organization and calm to an otherwise chaotic situation. The expected complaints, concerns and requests began to pour in, as many of my colleagues came from very distinguished careers and backgrounds, and they were under the same expectation that most are when they get to work at the White House. You know, things like matching furniture, unlimited resources and little delay of one's requests. This was where the experience came into play—I knew how to wheel and deal, and I knew that the secret to awesome furniture was scavenging the hallways of the building for discards. Believe it or not, you have to mix and match, and you are lucky when you have a conference table and chairs in your office. I was able to piece together most of everything everyone needed and requested.

We were off to a great start, because I worked tirelessly to ensure that the technology infrastructure was in place and ready within the first 72 hours as I had promised Ron that it would be. People had the technology resources and the fundamentals in place to serve our country, the administration and our newly elected vice president.

Speaking of the vice president, he and Dr. Biden were, of course, the highest priority when it came to providing them with their offices, their personal quarters at the Naval Observatory and a smooth transition from 36 years in the Senate and their lovely home in Delaware. It was apparent from day one that the Bidens cherished their time with their family more than probably anyone I have seen in elective office. It was not contrived nor for the cameras; it was this genuine affection and love that was shared among the Biden clan. One of my first "official" meetings with the vice president was an indoctrination in Joe Biden in many ways. Jovial, warm, effervescent but on point and focused. In our case, our topics were about his equipment needs, email information, telecommunication infrastructure and his and Dr. Biden's needs in relation to their offices and their new home. I learned very quickly and often teased the vice president that he must have been gay in a previous life, because his attention to detail when it came to carpeting, paint colors, the layout of a room and décor were better than mine and second to none. I met with him on several occasions, as he had very specific ideas and a vision, and he wanted to recreate his beloved rug colors and design from his Senate office. I did everything I could to accommodate his need to create an environment for him that was palatable, comfortable and worthy of our vice president.

On this subject, one of my favorite early recollections with Vice President Biden was when I received a call from Air Force Two. He was calling to request an armoire to go in his office—it had to have two doors so he could store his television in there but still fit the historic aspect of the vice president's office in the West Wing of the White House. In both of my White House tenures, the vice presidents themselves had an office just down the hall from the president in a beautiful and historic space with a fireplace and several windows overlooking West Executive Avenue, which is the private area between the executive office building and the White House itself. About 97% of the vice president's staff offices at the executive office building alongside the majority of the president's staff as well.

The vice president has one of the most ornate and stunning rooms in the White House complex in the executive office building that is at his disposal as a ceremonial room. It is the room that houses the desk that has been signed by vice presidents dating back decades. It always gave me great joy to take my guests or any of the vice president's guests to see this historic piece of furniture. The White House complex is made up of about 18 acres, and the entire compound is surrounded by a very secure perimeter that is guarded and managed by the U.S. Secret Service, as is common knowledge.

The actual pieces of furniture used in the West Wing for the most part are managed by the White House curator's office. It was such a pleasure when the request for the armoire reached my ears, because it required me to meet with the curator in the White House library, where Franklin Roosevelt conducted his now-famous fireside chats. The curator invited me to sit with him on a period piece from the colonial era that comfortably sat two people. As most people know, I am not a small fellow, and in typical Moe Vela style, I refused to sit on this museum piece because I was not entirely sure that it would hold me. He smiled and appreciated my concern but insisted that I sit down. I had a vision of my destroying like James Madison's parlor bench or something of the sort! The two-seat couch held up, thank goodness, and the curator was confident that he had just the right armoire for the vice president's use.

It was from approximately the early 1800s, if I recall, and had two doors and shelving inside that would hold the television perfectly. There was one major problem, though. He gave me a stern warning that nothing, absolutely nothing, was to be done to this historic armoire. I assured him that no one would touch the armoire except the television.

I arranged for the armoire to be delivered and installed exactly where Vice President Biden had requested—along the east wall of his office and within view of his desk so he could keep up with the breaking news in real time. It was installed over the weekend, and the vice president was elated on that Monday with its beauty. About on Wednesday of that week, I went over to the West Wing to make sure everything was still operating smoothly, not just with the armoire but with the three amazing assistants who sat outside his office as well. The vice president was on travel, so I went into his office and was so happy to see what a beautiful addition the armoire was to his office. I opened up the two old doors and I was horrified to find that a small hole had been drilled in the back of the armoire so that the television cord had a place to exit to the wall. I was absolutely certain that I was either going to be fired or at least never be welcomed in the curator's office again. Neither came to be true, obviously, but to this day, I'm not entirely sure who drilled the hole—but the vice president insists it was not him!

As for those three assistants outside the vice president's office, I learned 10 years before that they were the key to getting a meeting, a call or anything placed on the desk of the vice president. As with Vice President Gore, I was fortunate to have a great working relationship with the assistants who came with him from the Senate, Michelle Smith and Nancy Orloff. These ladies knew him well, and they knew his idiosyncrasies, patterns, likes and dislikes. Fundamentally, they knew how to handle him. After having served him in the Senate for several years, they knew his political relationships and, most importantly to the vice president, they knew his family and inner circle.

In addition to those key assistants, I came into the Obama-Biden White House knowing that the other key individual that needed to be operating on all cylinders at all times was the vice president's "body man," or the personal assistant who is at his side at all times except in very personal situations. In this case, it was a man named Fran Person. Frannie, as some of us affectionately refer to him, was a very tall drink of water who had played football at the University of South Carolina. It was apparent from minute number one that Fran was going to be a complete joy to work with—he was never demanding in his requests (which would typically come from the man himself), he never complained, he was respectful and kind and he never failed to share a warm smile and, in my case, an embrace. I grew to admire and genuinely love this guy, and that rapport Fran developed with everyone he encountered served the Bidens well over time. I don't want to imply that I was the only one who had this close working relationship with Frannie—I've never met anyone who did not feel the same way I do about this extraordinary human being.

I had equally developed a strong admiration and working relationship with the vice president's trip director, Sam Myers. Sam is a well-respected political operative who goes back many years with me in political circles. He is a gregarious and warm human being which represented the graciousness of the Biden's to a tee.

I also had my first encounter with our new second lady, which is a title that neither she nor anyone else really cares for, Dr. Jill Biden. I was only familiar with her from the television and news reports. As with most gay men and countless others, I had quietly admired her understated and classic elegance and beauty and was elated to finally meet her within my first week in the office. I met with her and Cathy Russell, her chief of staff, and I found Dr. Biden to be just as beautiful in person and equally warm, humble and gracious. She had a sparkle in her eyes, and I could tell that behind that genuine and down-to-earth persona laid a witty, fun and brilliant woman. I knew she was wicked smart, as today's Millennials say, and I found her to be nothing less than a joy from the get-go.

She redefines grace and graciousness. I love Jill Biden!

I felt for Dr. Biden, because she got one of the first glimpses of this new and improved Moe guy who returned a second time with a renewed confidence and sense of belonging. When I handled Tipper's office and management needs in the late 1990's I was younger and naïve and lacked self-confidence, so I was much more reserved and restrained. This time I came back with a vengeance! Not in any way arrogant or cocky—that would be a violation of my principles and upbringing—but confident. There is a fine line that I hope I have never crossed.

This confidence allowed me to relate to the Bidens in a much more human and collegial way. More like peers that I had the utmost respect for but not the underlying fear and insecurity that accompanied my first tenure in the White House. Let me be clear—any fear I have ever had in either tenure was rooted in respect, admiration and knowing my place. I have learned that it does not make me inferior or subservient to "know my place" in a conversation, setting or protocol situation; rather, it shows that I know what I'm doing. Rather than inject myself in a conversation for the sake of participating, I have learned to know when and how. This intuition combined with humility has served me well throughout my career.

I have too often watched my colleagues in these high-profile experiences who thought that yelling the loudest, complaining the most or finding the most fault in others would result in their advancement. More times than not, those people remained stagnant and stale and never became stellar. The key to this humility-based approach to life is that one must be on guard not to be perceived as weak or lacking in confidence—there is a fine line between being humble, grateful and knowing one's place, and weakness and lacking confidence.

I didn't need to change anything about myself in that first meeting with Dr. Biden, just like I refused to do with the vice president himself. It was blatantly clear then, and became even more apparent over the time we worked together, that the Bidens were extraordinarily special and rivaled the Liebermans in their sincerity, genuine being and heartfelt love. I remember vividly the moment I knew I would fall in love with Jill Biden during that first encounter. She and Cathy Russell, now Ambassador Russell, had a long list of items on their "priority requests" for their office.

If there was one very valuable lesson I learned with the Gores, it was if you keep the second lady or wife happy, the vice president tends to be happy! The last thing a vice president wants or needs after a long day in the West Wing with nuclear proliferation, terrorism threats, trade matters, immigration reform, healthcare, politics and domestic matters is an unhappy spouse when they arrive at the Naval Observatory. I was determined to get Cathy and Dr. Biden everything they needed. The toughest I ever saw Dr. Biden get in my relationship with her was on that day when she said, "Shake a tail feather." I knew we would become lifelong friends when I felt comfortable enough to stand up and shake my butt. We all laughed and I kissed and hugged her goodbye, and the makings of a great relationship were in place.

Several months into our tenure, and after all the years I had been involved in politics on the local, state and national levels, I was able to check one more thing off of my bucket list. Like so many Democrats and countless others around the world, I have always admired the Kennedys. As many say, they are as close to American royalty as we are going to get. Throughout my studies at the University of Texas in receiving my degree in government, the Kennedy legacy permeated much of my studies. As a young legislative aide in Texas and working on those various political campaigns, it was just understood that the Kennedys represented certain ideals, commitments and principles when it came to the poor, disenfranchised, powerless and voiceless, and they were ideals that I could relate to and that resonated with me.

As we all know from history, the only Kennedy we had left in public service from that generation was the Lion of the Senate, Ted Kennedy. I had never had the chance to meet Senator Kennedy, and it was always a dream of mine. In truth, the Kennedys tended to be much more liberal than I am in my politics, but, like I said, I admired them in so many ways. On an otherwise routine day in the White House, if there is such a thing, my desk phone rang. To my surprise, the call had mistakenly rolled over from the vice president's West Wing office to my desk. I said, as I usually do, "This is Moe." And the voice on the other end said, "This is Ted Kennedy, may I speak to Joe?" It is very rare for me to freeze, but that was one of those moments—not necessarily because it was Ted Kennedy, but more because the vice president's West Wing line had rolled over to me!

I composed myself and began what was to be a short but very meaningful conversation with Senator Kennedy. I advised him of the telecommunications mishap and informed him that the vice president was in the air returning from one of his frequent and often unannounced trips to Iraq. I assured him that I would have him call him upon his arrival. Before I let him go, though, I knew I had only one chance, since it was very public knowledge that Senator Kennedy was battling a cancerous brain tumor and had been declining in health. I mustered up the courage to say to him, "Senator, I'm from the Rio Grande Valley of Texas, Latino, raised Catholic and gay. I just want to take this chance to tell you how special you and your brothers are to me and so many other Latinos and gays. You are truly loved, and I'm not sure you are aware of this, but, Senator, to this day, it is not uncommon for traditional Latino families to have a picture of your brother, President Kennedy, right next to the picture of the Pope." I don't think I was hopefully imagining it, but there was a pep in his voice when he responded that warmed my heart. He said, "Moe, I know the Rio Grande Valley, and you are so kind to share those thoughts with me. They mean a lot to our family." I thought I would borrow just a few more minutes of American history and bid him farewell by telling him what Daddy would say often to people throughout my life. "Senator," I said, "I will tell you in Spanish what I wish for you. No se baje del caballo." He responded without hesitation and said, "I'm not going to stop riding this horse until it knocks me off." We hung up, and I bowed my head and wept silently at my desk. The senator passed away a few months later after a courageous battle with cancer, and our country lost yet another Kennedy who made such a huge difference in the lives of so many of us.

Within the first year of my time with the Bidens, through everything from accommodating the need for bunk beds at the house for their beloved grandchildren at the Naval Observatory to ensuring that the vice president had a physical trainer that he enjoyed to directing all the more serious budgetary, operational, administrative and management matters that I had to conduct on a daily basis, I grew closer and closer to the Bidens.

During that first year, I noticed that they were scheduled to go to Chile and Costa Rica on an official trip. Once again, not being a novice came into play. I knew well enough that if you wanted to participate, you had to ask. People's lives were so hectic, and the planning and details of these types of trips were complicated, time-consuming and intense. I requested to go as the senior-most Latino on the staff, and my request was granted.

Returning to ride in the staff van, arriving at Andrews Air Force Base, pulling up to Air Force Two and boarding those steps into history as an older and wiser man made it even that much more poignant for me. I had goose bumps all over again. It never got old. It was a relatively long flight, and we had to stop to refuel on the way down in San Jose, Costa Rica. En route, the Bidens were their consistent selves in coming out of their cabin to mingle andlaugh with all of us. As in previous years, those times on Air Force Two are a time that you truly get to know one another in a more informal and personal sense. It was on that first leg that I had a beautiful conversation with Vice President Biden about his devout Catholic faith. I shared with him that he and my father shared that conviction and a special devotion to the Virgin Mary. He was visibly touched by that story, as was I, and it was even more significant when several years later and after I had left my service to him, he and his incredible sister, Valerie, brought me back a rosary that was blessed by the Pope during their visit to the Vatican. Although I left the Catholic church many years ago because I tired of hearing of how I was wrong, bad and going to burn in hell for who I was, the gesture from the Bidens impacted me in a deeply meaningful way. I will cherish that rosary for the rest of my journey.

On that trip, I also experienced two other Air Force Two "firsts." The refueling stop in Costa Rica was a strange experience in that our able and talented Air Force pilots pulled up to a private terminal on the outskirts of what I think was the San Jose airport. For some reason, we had to wait a couple of hours before taking off again for the final leg of the trip to Santiago, Chile. We literally sat on the tarmac with the doors of Air Force Two all opened and a comfortable Costa Rican breeze filling the plane for the entire two to three hours. It was the oddest sensation, and I felt like I was in a movie!

The second first-time experience was in our final approach to Santiago, Chile. I have been saying for years that there was not enough money in the world for me to be a pilot. I'm scared of heights, and my vision is horrific at best. Some of the most incredible members of our armed forces serve the president and vice president in so many capacities, including flying and managing Air Force One and Two. On my numerous flights in both administrations, I have experienced nothing less than incomparable hospitality, the utmost professionalism and welcoming smiles. Every service member on any flight went out of their way to make us all feel welcomed and comfortable. This flight was no exception.

Much to my surprise, the vice president asked me if I had ever sat in the cockpit of Air Force Two in my previous experiences, and I informed him that was one thing I had not experienced. He asked if I wanted to sit up there with the pilots, and I jumped at the chance. The pilots were tremendously warm and jovial. They eased my fears immediately. My biggest fear at that point was not sitting in the cockpit nor seeing the landing from a completely different perspective nor even the fact that it was Air Force Two that I was doing this in, but that the damn harness seat belt in the cockpit was not going to close around my big belly! The guys up front laughed with me and assured me that it would not prevent me from experiencing the awe. They tugged on the harness as I sucked in as far as I could until that thing snapped shut. It was truly euphoric as I listened on my headset as they communicated with the control tower in Santiago, and they would describe for me how they identified the runway below. I soaked in every minute of it. It was nighttime, and the lights of Santiago and the runway looked magical. I will never forget those words: "Air Force Two coming in for landing."

While the vice president and some of my colleagues attended official meetings with President Bachelet and others, I had the privilege of spending time with Dr. Biden and her staff. Many of the meetings were held in the coastal town of Vina del Mar, and it was there that I knew Dr. Biden had become my friend when she cautioned me that I was eating way too many carbohydrates at the meals we had shared. I love her for watching out for me, and I sadly continue to disappoint her, I am sure, on that front.

After everyone was in their respective rooms on one particular night, I decided to walk around this charming coastal town and came upon a beautiful casino. It was memorable to walk in there and play 3-card poker when I realized I was at the table with almost our entire Secret Service detail. It was bonding, and I most definitely felt safer the rest of the trip.

On many of these trips, it is not uncommon for the wife of the vice president to have a separate itinerary than the vice president himself, unless there are events that require them to both be present. Sometimes the events are more official in nature, such as meetings with local non-profits or NGOs, and others can involve visiting cultural or art exhibits, sightseeing and meeting with the locals to create good will. One cannot go to Chile without tasting their world-class wine. I was fortunate that the Chilean government thought it important that Dr. Biden and her team get a tour of a typical Chilean vineyard and a sample or two or three of their best exports. All I'm going to say is that the Chilean wine was exquisite and that the way home on Air Force Two was comical when the overhead bin space was a lot more limited due to the cases and cases of wine we brought back with us. I'm not going to lie; some of it did not make it all the way back home!

We were in Santiago on a Sunday, and one of my fondest memories of my tenure with the Bidens was when the vice president asked me if I would attend Mass with him and a few of my colleagues in a Catholic church in a park-like setting. Again, I had left the church many years ago, but attending Mass with Vice President Biden was special for me. I was able to put aside my disdain for the Catholic Church for that hour in time as I prayed alongside of him and was inspired by his deep and abiding faith.

It was not the first time I had attended Mass with a sitting vice president of the United States, as back in the late 1990s, during a visit to Los Angeles, I accompanied Vice President Gore to Mass at the Cathedral. As he sat with Hispanic union leaders and I alongside them, all I recall from that experience was that when the collection basket came around, it was me who had to provide Vice President Gore with the $20 bill to place in the basket. Now that I share that story, I realize that I never got my money back!

We began our way back to the United States, but not before we stopped in San Jose, Costa Rica. I had not been to Chile nor Costa Rica, so I was elated to see two new countries and add them to my travel portfolio. We stayed at a charming hotel in the outskirts of San Jose that was set among what felt a little like a Tarzan movie in a jungle setting, as I recall. It was lovely, calming and relaxing. Once again, the vice president had his high-level meetings with that country's leadership, and I accompanied Dr. Biden and my colleagues as she visited a local elementary school.

I'm so glad we had built a strong relationship by then, because I actually did what no staff member is ever to do. The Costa Rican school children sang a beautiful song to welcome her and all of us to their school which was in a horrible state of disrepair. There were open-air classrooms as is traditional in the climate of Costa Rica, but the challenges their school faced did not deter nor adversely affect their ability to smile, love and enjoy their educational experience. We visited a classroom, and it is there that I engaged in a faux pas.

When you staff a Principal, as we refer to the president, first lady, vice president and second lady, you are never to interfere with them being the center of attention. You must always stay out of the press pictures and limelight if at all possible. This classroom of poor and humble Costa Rican school children tugged at my Latino heartstrings. I saw in them my community and my heritage as a Hispanic, and it brought back memories of parts of my home area and the northern border of Mexico. I was moved and touched by their cherubic faces and started to squat down next to them and speak to them in Spanish. I inquired about their families and what subjects they enjoyed the most. All good and heartfelt, but I was NOT the second lady of the United States. All this time, poor Dr. Biden, who doesn't speak Spanish, was trying to carry out her duties, and I was getting the attention.

I was fortunate that Jill Biden is the least pretentious person I think I have ever met. She and my colleagues found humor in the situation and ribbed me about it for months after that trip. If I'm not mistaken, the picture the next day in the Costa Rican press was of Jill Biden and me talking to students. I clearly had a lapse in judgment and let my emotions get the best of me. It was not a fatal mistake by any stretch of the imagination; it was innocent, and I hope I actually contributed to the good will created by that visit, but it was a reminder that we must use our heart and mind in coordination and never one without the other, as Ann Richards taught me when I was about 21 years old. In hindsight, I'm proud that I knew my place and was not seeking the limelight but was acting from my heart—and that makes it much more easily forgiven.

We returned to Washington, D.C. with stories to tell, and my job of managing the daily operations of the office of the vice president continued. At that year's annual Cinco de Mayo event at the Naval Observatory, Alan Hoffman, one of my colleagues , granted me the tremendous honor of introducing the Bidens to the guests that included distinguished Latino leaders and others from around the country. It was so meaningful to me to have that opportunity, because it gave me a small but beautiful chance to show my fellow community leaders how the Bidens valued Latinos on their team, how they respected our community and how they were just like us in so many ways.

My distant cousin, Carlos Elizondo, who went to high school with me in Harlingen, Texas, had become the Bidens' social secretary, the role Philip Dufour had played for the Gores years before. It was amazing to have family and a dear friend from the same little town in south Texas on the team as well. What are the odds of that? Additionally, the only other person who, like Ron Klain and I, had served on the Gore team, Anthony Bernal, was our other senior Hispanic, as he was deputy chief of staff to Dr. Biden. Imagine, three senior Latinos, and all gay to top it all off! What a statement and message that alone sends about Ron Klain and the Bidens.

I introduced the Bidens from the landing of the main staircase in the vice president's residence. It was there that I shared with the guests what I had shared with the Bidens privately many times before in relation to Latino events. The vice president, as most know, comes from a close-knit Irish-Catholic family and was raised in working-class neighborhoods in Scranton, PA and Wilmington, DE. I told the audience that night that he was no different than we as Hispanics. I knew this because I had worked closely by his side and I had gotten to know his heart and mind. He, as an Irish-Catholic, shares our Latino values— love of country, faith, family and community. These values created an inextricable bond between him and our community. The vice president went on to deliver his typical heartfelt remarks, and the lovefest between America, Hispanics and Joe Biden grew one level deeper and stronger.

At one of these wonderful events at the vice president's residence that my cousin, Carlos, managed so perfectly, I had an encounter with a woman who has become very special to me. This woman was dressed impeccably, laughed freely and was approachable due to her engaging charm. It was not until 10 to 15 minutes into this delightful conversation with this bubbly blond did I realize that I was talking to Valerie Biden Owens, the vice president's best friend and sister. Val, as I now affectionately call her, is just slightly behind Jill when it comes to who influences the vice president the most. These two ladies are his confidantes and advisors, and Val ran his two presidential campaigns as well as , most, if not all of his senatorial campaigns. It was during that encounter that the story got even more intriguing.

I started realizing, as I was enthralled in our conversation and laughter, that I had met this lady before. That feeling can be somewhat haunting when you can't quite remember where and when. Then it came to me all at once. The night of the first

Inaugural Ball, another cousin and I decided to attend the LGBT Inaugural Ball, and it was held at the Mayflower Hotel. We engaged in a nightcap after the event in the lobby bar. Anyone who knows me knows that I am my father's son and will talk to anyone at a table within arm's length, and at bus stops, on airplanes and trains and anywhere else for that matter. That night was no different, and we had befriended the people at the table next to us. It was a group of about eight people. We all had on tuxedos and ball gowns, as there were events around the city, as we were all experiencing the high of this historic inauguration.

I'm not sure why I remember this—I rarely drink, but I had consumed a few apple martinis (I did say I was gay, okay). In passing, I shared with these lovely people at the table next to us, how extra special this night was to me because I had come back to serve my country again and make a little bit of American history. They all got a very interesting look on their faces. They asked me what role I was going to play, and I told them I was going to be Vice President Biden's director of management and administration. Laughter ensued as the lady said, "I'm Valerie Biden Owens, and this is my husband, Jack, and several members of the Biden family." We all hugged and found that chance encounter entertaining.

The reconnection with Val that evening at the Naval Observatory has resulted in a cherished friendship. Her sense of humor and style are larger than life—she truly lights up a room when she enters. She's a Biden through and through, as she goes through life with the confidence, trust, heart and ear of the vice president of the United States accompanied with that trademark Biden humility, faith and gratitude.

Valerie Biden Owens on the left—she arranged for the Bidens to take this memorable picture with many Velas.

In my current role as the owner of a business development consulting firm, I was in Santa Barbara, California last year meeting with a potential client. As is often the case, the potential client referenced my service to the Bidens with a sense of awe and respect. He went on to tell me he had a Biden story. I hear that so frequently as I travel across the nation, and it is a direct reflection of what I call the Biden effect. This particular gentleman went on to admit, in front of his wife, no less, that he had a crush on a Biden once upon a time because she was the "hottest" teacher he had. He proceeded to inform me that the subject of his crush was none other than Valerie Biden and that he would just sit in class and daydream about how pretty she was as his 8th grade art teacher. I promptly texted Val in front of the gentleman, because I knew it would bring her joy and warm her heart. Her response was so reflective of her incredible sense of humor as she said, "I was hot—and I still am!" I love that lady, and, yes, she's still got it.

As I previously mentioned, I came back the second time to serve, clearly not for the money with the 72% cut in pay, but because the commitment to serve overpowered all else. My salary for the second experience was only about $4,000 more than I made the first time. This time I was making $100,000. When Ron asked me to do this, he knew I would be making a tremendous sacrifice, but he also knew how committed I was to him, the Latino and gay communities, public service and my country. What many folks don't know is that the vice president's office has two budgets that each sustain around 65 full-time employees. The vice president gets a budget as one of several offices within the White House or office of the president and then gets another budget as president of the United States Senate. Most senior officials, like me, would be making substantially more money in the private sector. You truly do it because you care. However, I made an enormous mistake after the first time in the White House, and I vowed I would not make it again.

Many of my former colleagues in the Clinton-Gore White House leveraged and parlayed their roles into major money-making careers. Several of them ran for office and won mayoral, gubernatorial or other races around the country. Several of them took on high-profile corporate roles. No one had ever taught me what it was to parlay and leverage an experience or a job into an advancement in one's career. Frankly, it never crossed my mind, as I was just so humbled and grateful for the opportunity that had been presented to me that I would not dare think of how I would gain from it in those days. I truly walked the halls in the Clinton-Gore days just in awe and in an almost out-of-body experience. The future was not a thought, and I paid the price in some ways.

I don't regret my tenures and life experiences in Birmingham, San Diego and Denver in any way, shape or form. To the contrary, they are all reasons I am who I am today and have learned the lessons that sustain me as a thought leader, entrepreneur and man. On this second adventure I was determined to serve with no less humility and gratitude but with confidence and a cognizance of the future. I often am asked to advise and mentor Millennials and others and I tell them not to make the mistake I made and to remember that every relationship you make today may play a role in your future. Every relationship has value—you just might not find out what it is for years to come, so make them, nurture them, enhance them and let them grow.

As part of this more self-assured approach to my service, I decided that I was given a unique platform through my role in the vice president's office to educate, inform and inspire those around me through my actions, words and deeds. In returning the second time, I came to find out that I had a much more interactive and direct role with the military leaders assigned to the vice president's office. The vice president is assigned military aides who travel and accompany him everywhere he goes: a military doctor, military personnel to drive the fleet of cars, the military members who handle all aspects of the Naval Observatory and several others. They are of various ranks, and, in both White Houses, they were a daily reminder of the remarkable service our military provides our nation and the many sacrifices they and their families incur for our safety and freedom. Being raised by a Korean War veteran, it didn't take my two tenures in the White House to develop my profound passion and advocacy for our military and veterans. Several of those military service members that I served with are still friends to this day. Those are embraces that are doubly meaningful to me.

I decided that since I had to meet with several military officers more frequently in this tenure than the previous one that I would use that opportunity to enlighten, break down barriers and move a step closer to equality in my small and limited way. I'm no sociologist or psychologist by any stretch of the imagination—as a matter of fact, I probably need the services of the latter like most of us do—but I used our meetings as a platform to conduct an experiment.

First and foremost, I started every meeting (not just with the military folks, but with anyone I met with) by asking how they and their loved ones were doing. If it was a Monday, I asked about their weekend. If there was a holiday, I asked how they celebrated it. If was Christmas, spring break or summertime, I asked about their children, families and travel plans. I also made it a point to use the word LOVE at least once in every meeting. The first few times I did this experiment, you could see the discomfort around the table. Men would adjust their ties and collars; women would squirm in their seats. It was amazing to witness how "humanizing" the workplace created such disturbance.

If not in meetings, I made it a point to start each and every day by walking the halls and checking in on all of my colleagues: asking them similar questions about their lives; assuring them that I was there for them as a resource; and subtly reminding them not to lose sight of their own mental, physical, emotional and spiritual health while these jobs could be all-consuming.

The many months of these types of meetings and office visits resulted in some of the most meaningful working relationships

I have ever experienced. The communication levels improved, the collaborations were much more effective and the outcomes were working relationships built on mutual respect, trust and warmth. I would like to think that this little effort went a long way in breaking down barriers, building on our commonalities, celebrating our differences and creating a cohesive workforce that better served the vice president and our nation.

Right by my side in all of those efforts were my two incredible assistants, Zach Klein and Jillian Doody. They were loyal and trusted colleagues, and I cherish our time in the trenches together. Like many Millennials before them and after them, I am proud that I have always taken the time to mentor and guide any younger person who wants to learn from my mistakes or gain some wisdom from the little I have accomplished. Zach and Jilly, as I call her, were the epitome of confidence with humility, loyalty and respect. We cried and we laughed, and we got the job done.

There is a great lesson to be learned about why it is vital to love, respect and treat all people with basic human dignity. You just don't know today what a person may become or where they may end up tomorrow. Case in point, I met Zach Klein many years before when he was doing a semester of study in our nation's capital when he was a student at Ohio State University. I was honored to be a guest lecturer to his class one fateful day during the end of my Gore tenure.

Zach kept in touch with me for several years after that, and I watched him develop and grow up to be an incredible man, husband and father. When Ron Klain convinced me to come back to serve, I knew who I wanted as my deputy. I called Zach, and he sacrificed like I did and came to serve his country. It's vital to make meaningful and genuine relationships on this journey, as today I beam with pride as if it was my little brother while Zach dutifully serves the people of Columbus, Ohio as the president of the city council.

I am hopeful that through the non-stop media coverage of our president and vice president and their respective families, the American people have come to see the authenticity, honesty and transparency that is the Biden family. As we all saw with profound sadness, the Bidens lost a very special part of their family unit in Beau's passing. We, as a nation, mourned, grieved and suffered with them as they were forced to publicly say goodbye to this exemplary father, husband, son, brother, nephew, friend and public servant. As we have all read about for years, the vice president's resolve, faith and resiliency has been tested so many times on his journey—from the loss of his first wife and infant daughter to his own near-death health challenges to the loss of Beau. This man is truly remarkable in how he has handled adversity and loss with such grace.

I attended Beau's funeral Mass in Wilmington, DE. It was at once the most beautiful tribute to a great man and also emotionally taxing as one watched the anguish in the eyes of the vice president and the entire Biden family. My heart still aches for them. Once again, even in the worst of circumstances, the Bidens demonstrated to our nation the true meaning of family and devotion. My experience with the Bidens was extraordinary. I am one of the luckiest men alive in that I am able to truly call two vice presidents and their wives my personal and good friends.

CHAPTER THIRTEEN

INTERESTINGLY, MY EXPERIENCE IN THE OBAMA WHITE HOUSE itself and outside the office of the vice president was somewhat different to the fond memories of the Clinton-Gore White House. Unlike the warmth and humility one found in the halls of the Clinton White House, I found some members of the Obama team cold, entitled, aloof and distant.

Serving among the Obama team was starting to make it clear that there might be something to all the references I had heard about how the people from the South were different from those from the Midwest. Like so many have seen in movies, TV shows, books and reality, there is a certain charm, congeniality and approachability among Southerners. I'm not in any way suggesting that the sins of the Southern past should be forgotten, nor do I mean to paint them out to be ideal in every way. I'm merely contrasting the air of arrogance I found in the mostly Midwestern/ Chicago Obama hallways with the graciousness and friendliness of the Arkansas Clinton hallways. There was a dramatic difference. I will be criticized for sharing this observation, but I know there are many who share my sentiments—they might just not have the courage, or stupidity, to tell the truth.

Much like the Clintons themselves, I greatly admire the Obamas. I have had limited interaction with all four of them but have been around them multiple times and found them all to be brilliant, warm and funny. I admire all of them greatly. In my comparisons of the two White House environments, I am in no way suggesting that those four Principals are personally what I experienced or observed—although I can't deny that in most corporate settings, as in the White House, the tone and ambiance is set by the CEO, in this case the president himself. I am convinced that what I observed in the aloof behavior of some of his top aides was not completely nor truly reflective of him as much as it was reflective of those individuals as products of their environments. It is very clear that President Obama is cerebral and more guarded of his emotions, but it is equally clear that he is a passionate, kind and well-meaning man. I am absolutely certain that what I was probably experiencing and sensing was less of an arrogance and aloofness and more of a lack of appreciation from some members of the Obama team as to the fact that I had not worked on the campaign. In other words, I was an "outsider."

A good example of my observations occurred in a meeting with several senior Obama folks from the White House. It was a meeting to discuss the president and vice president's policy priorities among ethnic and niche groups such as African Americans, Hispanics, LGBT, women, etc. There were a couple dozen of us in the room around a very large table. After some initial roundtable discussions, I spoke up. I introduced myself and said which office I was from. I went on to explain that my thoughts in preparing to advocate for healthcare reform were that we should not reinvent the wheel. I shared my experience in that when we did any policy initiative in the Clinton White House, we would put out all types of material about how our policy initiative would effect and impact a particular niche group.

For example, we might put out a one-pager on how welfare reform impacted single moms or the crime bill impacted Hispanics. No sooner did I finish my thoughts than I was shut down by a senior Obama official who bluntly and curtly said, "Moe, you clearly did not understand the mandate of this election. Barack has proven that we are One America and we don't need to engage in the niche approaches of the past."

I knew that minute that this was going to be an interesting experience. I drank the Kool-Aid and I believed in the hope and change that was promised, but this was not my first rodeo, like most of them. I still knew in my gut—and that's a lot of intuition if you know the size of my gut—that my two communities were still going to require the nuanced attention and communication and respect they deserved and sought. It was not about niche segmentation; it was about knowing that our society is not monolithic and that we still have cultural differences, nuances, patterns and idiosyncrasies. The Obama administration started off with a very limited niche outreach program in their office of public engagement, but they sure did have to adjust as they saw how divided our nation truly remained, and their reelection efforts were a clear indication that their "hopey changey" One America was not as much of a reality as they had imagined..

I will never forget a particular sunny afternoon as I was sitting in my massive office in the Eisenhower Executive Office Building In every other way it was an ordinary one. However,

Jillian poked her head in and advised me that there was a presidential intern that was interested in seeing me. I have always had an open-door policy regardless of my title or role, so I welcomed them to join me on the couch in my office. What I heard next truly broke my heart.

Before me sat a very handsome young man with sad eyes. At moments, his eyes would fill with tears and emotion as he described for me the painful experience of being the first transgendered intern in the White House internship program. The office to which he had been assigned was not reflective of the "hope" and "change" that the president envisioned and promised, as he had been subjected to disenfranchisement. I literally held that intern in my arms and told him that I would do everything in my power to have him transferred into an environment where he was welcomed, loved and celebrated. I did just that.

I have said for years that even many of us in the LGBT community have not fully understood the struggles and challenges of our transgendered brothers and sisters. In reality, most of us from the progressive persuasion have simply been politically correct in our support of their efforts. On that day, that intern inspired me to make a concerted effort to truly attempt to understand gender dysphoria. Within 18 months of that intern's painful story, I had the privilege of sitting on the GLAAD board with one of our nation's most brilliant transgendered Americans, Jenny Boylan. She is a highly respected English professor and published author. Through some meaningful conversations with Jenny, I was able to continue my educational and insightful initiative into the livesof the transgendered. At the end of the day, I came to realize that I didn't even need to understand their plight, although I have a much stronger insight than ever before, but that as a gay man, as a Latino, as a chubby man, as a man who wears glasses, all I need to understand is that all of us as human beings are equal and should be afforded respect and basic human dignity.

I don't want to be completely negative in comparing the two White Houses, because of my deep admiration for the Obamas, but there is another example of when entitlement and arrogance can be a deterrence to progress. Again, the Clinton White House operation and infrastructure was rooted in this sentiment of service and opportunity. If you had the privilege of meeting Bill Clinton, you knew from the handshake and the eye contact that man had a unique ability to "feel" you and "get" you and was for you. He was entrancing, and that feeling that he was a champion of the people set the stage of his White House. He was remarkably accessible and approachable as well. I attribute this to his upbringing and life experiences in Arkansas. I share all of this because what I saw in the communications shop of the Clinton White House was the same approachability and accessibility you felt with President Clinton himself.

On the reverse side, the Obama White House communications efforts seemed to be caught off-guard from day one.. I'm not entirely sure that they were ever out front of a story in the entire first term. They were forced to play defense consistently and, like a good Texan, I know that offense is the one that usually results in points. It was frustrating to sit in my office among these people and watch when I had been so fortunate to see such an effective team the first time around.

My frustration continued to mount as I felt the wrath and non-inclusive spirit of some of the President's folks. It was not just the senior folks—my fellow Hispanic who were on the Obama team were, at times, the greatest culprits of this behavior pattern. It was no secret that I had not worked on the campaign, and they were going to make sure I paid the price. Things had changed since I last served, and I naively thought that I would encounter the same camaraderie and collegiality that I experienced on my first go around, but I was sadly mistaken.

With the same good intentions and willingness to serve as the first time, no sooner did we get started in that first term than I reached out to some of the president's top Hispanic advisors. I recommended to them that we call a meeting of all Hispanic staff members in the White House so we could coordinate and work as a unit so that our community was represented, and more importantly, so that the president and vice president could be better served. They begrudgingly agreed to co-host the meeting with me. After all, this is what Maria Echeveste, Mickey Ibarra, Janet Murguia, Susana Valdez, Cynthia Jasso Rotunno and several others and I did throughout our service together in the Clinton White House—it was effective then, and I was confident it would be effective again.

Regrettably, whether it was their egos or insecurities, or maybe I was just too much of a threat to their newfound perches of power, they made it impossible for me to lend my leadership to their efforts. History would repeat itself, as it was my fellow Hispanic who would call and speak ill of me to Ron Klain in an effort to weaken my leadership and role. I have chosen not to name this particular person because, frankly, the president's record on Latino issues, especially immigration reform, and the massive number of deportations and Latino families destroyed, has been dismal and speaks for itself. Unfortunately, it is a lack of leadership by this particular person who blocked and denigrated me on whose watch it fell short. History will not be kind to them on this particular issue. Most Hispanics will remain silent on this matter and even criticize me for speaking out because they don't want to risk not being invited to the White House holiday and other political events, but I think it is time for us to hold people accountable even if it is someone from our own community or someone we love and respect.

The life lesson for me, as I discuss in much more detail in a later chapter, is that my fellow Hispanics were just not going to be the primary source of support in my career. I was determined not to let their behavior toward me ever keep me from serving my community, including them, loving them and respecting them.

As it was quickly demonstrated that I was not going to be effective in participating on a macro level in the Obama White House, I resigned myself and poured my heart into the awesome and wonderful Biden world. It was truly life-altering to work with the Bidens, and my colleagues on the vice president's team were nothing less than amazing. So many of them went on to serve in other capacities and undoubtedly will become corporate titans, run foundations, NGOs and think tanks and run for office. Whatever they decide to do, they will be great at it, and the bond we created during those first years of the Obama administration will once again last a lifetime. As for the Bidens, much like the Gores, they have remained personal friends. I cherish the opportunities and memories. I celebrate them as human beings, and I honor their service to our nation.

I truly hold no grudge against anyone on the Obama team. Those are tough jobs surrounded by enormous stress. I just feel fortunate that I got to work with a Clinton team that was so positive and inclusive, and with two vice presidents and their teams, wives and families; my beloved chief of staff both times, Ron Klain; and my indomitable colleagues and friends in both offices of the vice president who were beyond amazing.

CHAPTER FOURTEEN

LIFE IN THE BIDEN WORLD WAS NOTHING SHORT OF AMAZING for me. With the confidence that accompanied me due to age, life experience and familiarity with the job, I walked the halls with my shoulders back, head held high and knowing I belonged. . The Bidens brought back that magical feeling again with their open and inclusive spirit and the environment they created for us.

Once I got past the fact that I would not be allowed to contribute on the President's team, I focused on my daily responsibilities and enjoyed the ride. It was great the second time around to realize that I still gave a "mean" West Wing tour, and I was just as passionate about sharing that experience with as many people as I possibly could. I think in the 16 months or so that I served this second time, I gave close to 100 tours—some of the most memorable West Wing tours of my life, actually. Somehow I had gained a reputation of giving an extra-animated and intriguing tour. Imagine that—Moe Vela, the gay guy who tried to make it on Broadway, giving an animated West Wing tour!

My colleagues could have been patronizing me by asking me frequently to give their tours "because you are so much better than me," but I think the real reason was that I was a sucker and that they didn't want to stay past 7:00 p.m. after a long day of work!

Regardless, I gave them with all the energy I could muster after those long hours. One of my colleagues whom I adore, Courtney O' Donnell, who is now a senior executive at AirBnB, called me on what would have been any other day. I knew she had two young boys at home, so I quickly agreed to substitute for her so she could get home to them. All she said was, "It's some Hollywood types."

I was intrigued but, frankly, the day had been so busy that by the time I went to meet them at the Southwest Gate, where we meet our tour guests, I had forgotten about the Hollywood part. If I remember correctly, , it was an extra late tour, and I went to retrieve them at around 9:00 p.m. We got the three of them through the magnetometers and Secret Service screening, and I began to walk north up West Executive Avenue as we headed to the door of the West Wing.

My customary presentation at this stage of the tour involved turning their attention to the ornate, stately and stunning façade of the Eisenhower Executive Office Building to our left. I explained how it housed the vast majority of the president's staff, national security teams, operations, the VP ceremonial office and the infamous bowling alley. I realized as we approached the West Wing entry that I, nor did I know them from appearance. I can't lie, I was a little disappointed that it wasn't Meryl Streep or Morgan Freeman, but I obliged and gave them one of my "animated" tours.

As we entered the west door to the West Wing, they took pictures, like most people do, with the presidential seal behind them on the awning, and they stopped to enjoy the pictures of the Obamas, Bidens and their families that the White House photographer places along the walls of the West Wing. Those pictures are continuously refreshed with pictorials of recent events and travels of the Principals and even Bo and Sunny. Up to this point, I just knew that my guests' names were Naomi, Doug and Janet.

I finally decided to inquire a little further as we were approaching the White House Mess. The Hollywood trio informed me that they were actually doing some informal research for a movie they were making about the Valerie Plame story, the CIA operative who was allegedly "outed" as a result of Vice President Cheney's staff. It turned out that Naomi was Naomi Watts, the A-list beautiful Australian actress; Doug was Doug Liman, the director of the *Bourne Identity* trilogy, *Mr. and Mrs. Smith*, *Jumper* and several other successful films; and Janet was Janet Zucker, the wife and production partner of Jerry Zucker, the acclaimed writer and director of *Naked Gun*, *Airplane* and *Ghost*, among others.

I got a pep in my step as they started to share Hollywood stories with me. After I explained, as we stood at the door of the White House mess, that only senior staff had memberships and pointed out the White House china on the tables, I turned around to notice that Naomi Watts and Janet Zucker were no longer with us. This is a West Wing tour guide's worst nightmare, as it can result in you never getting to give another tour or, in really serious violations, removal of your badge or worse. My heart skipped a beat. At the other end of this short hall, I noticed Naomi and Janet knocking on a door. My life and career flashed before my eyes. It was probably the ONLY room, other than the Oval Office, that a guest or staff member could not and should not knock on.

The ladies were knocking on the door of the Situation Room, the famously secretive enclave where the highest levels of security clearance are required. To my horror, a young national security operative answered the door before I could tell them to please back away and move on. The handsome and strapping young man took two seconds, and all I heard was, "Naomi Watts, is that you?"

The next thing I knew we were all invited in to a portion of the room, and the star-struck man shared what he was allowed to share with us and not violate any rules. Honestly, once the fear momentarily left me, the four of us were in awe. We actually stayed in there for over an hour, but it felt like 20 hours to me as I kept trying everything without being rude to get them the hell out of there.

We continued on our tour up the West Wing stairs to the magnificent and awe-inspiring Oval Office, Roosevelt Room, West Wing lobby and beautiful Rose Garden. We finished, as we tended to do, in the White House press briefing room, where, during the Clinton days, our guests could take a picture behind the same podium and White House seal that the president's press secretary and the president himself use frequently.

By the time I returned for my Obama White House days, we were no longer allowed to let folks take a picture at the podium, since the backdrop and podium had been replaced during the Bush years and there was a concerted effort to protect this costly renovation. It was always one of my favorite parts of the tour, but it was still fun to make our guests aware that we were standing on what used to be Franklin Roosevelt's indoor solarium/ pool. Below the White House press briefing room that one sees on television is the shell of the pool, which now houses rows and rows of wires and cables.

By the end of this "Hollywood" tour, Janet Zucker and I, in particular, had bonded, and I could tell a friendship had been struck. She introduced me to the one and only Jerry Zucker the next day, and they remain very dear friends to this day.

As a matter of fact, we are in the development phase of a television show together that was an idea of mine, and it is mesmerizing to work with them and learn from them of an industry that is new to me. The Zuckers were so grateful that I gave them and their guests the West Wing tour that Jerry asked me if I wanted to have a cameo role in the movie they were shooting in Washington, D.C. The movie was called *Fair Game*, and the scene I'm in was filmed at the Willard Hotel on a dark and cloudy morning. It happened to be the morning I was to leave with the Bidens to Chile and Costa Rica. If you blink, you will miss me as I exit the revolving main door as Sean Penn's character enters the building. It might last less than one second, but it didn't end up on the cutting room floor, as they say in Hollywood!

Little did I know, that West Wing tour would not be my last brush with Hollywood in this second White House experience. Truthfully, I was so fortunate to attend many events that included celebrities of film and stage, musicians and entertainers and heads of state. One never loses the giddiness and tingles you get when you around someone you watched on TV or at the movie theater or listened to on your headphones, but you become more accustomed over time and are able to contain yourself. The key was to not embarrass the Principals in those instances, nor yourself for that matter.

On yet another routine day, or as routine as a day can be when you are employed at the White House, a colleague called and used the "you give such a better tour than me" line, and I fell for it yet again. This time, though, I couldn't believe my eyes when I realized who I was retrieving at the Southwest Gate. By this point in my career, I truly didn't get star struck, but this particular guest was testing my diplomacy skills.

As I approached the gate, once again I didn't even bother to check the names of who I was taking through—I was exhausted, it was 8:00 p.m. and I just wanted to be a gracious host and go home. As I walked up to the gate, I noticed Rob Lowe standing there with another gentleman and two teenage boys. I was certain that was not my tour. Fortunately, it was my tour.

Rob, his son, his son's friend and the friend's father introduced themselves. They were all four delightful, warm and approachable from the get-go. They were on spring break with their sons, and they thought a tour of the West Wing was in order. If you have not connected the dots, the West Wing has a special connotation to Rob Lowe—he was a star on the *The West Wing*, the award-winning and popular television show, so giving him an actual West Wing tour was extra poignant.

Ironically, during the Los Angeles Democratic Convention, one of the many activities that I took the Lieberman family to was a private tour of the set of *The West Wing*. I shared this co-incidence with Rob, and we reminisced. It dawned on me as we were approaching the west entry door to the West Wing that he would know a great deal about what we were about to see, since the set was a very realistic recreation of the actual West Wing.

Rob Lowe tried very hard throughout the tour to let me give my "animated" tour and even complimented me on several oc-casions for the interesting trivia and historic references. It was one of my proudest moments to hear Rob say, "I actually didn't know that." During our tour and in the middle of one of our many conversations, I was made aware that the next day was Rob's birthday. I was sure he had a booked schedule and full day planned, but I thought it would be a nice gesture on behalf of the administration, to host him for lunch in the White House mess.

I was so fortunate in both administrations to have an account and be a member of the White House mess, as I tried to share that experience with as many people as possible as well. Having a mess account is an incredible privilege, and no cash or credit is exchanged, so the account holder is provided a monthly bill and has to pay their monthly invoice out of their personal funds. I re-member months where my heart and generosity got the most of me as I hosted friends and family to experience the joy of seeing their eyes light up to be eating on White House china, only to get this enormous bill and wonder how the hell I was going to pay for it in light of my 72% cut in pay!

Surprisingly, Rob rearranged his schedule and was very touched by the birthday lunch invitation for him and his son.

The White House mess always accommodated, and this was no exception. They were just as excited at having Rob Lowe in the quaint and small dining room as anyone else, so they were more than happy to oblige when I asked them to bake him a last-minute birthday cake. Rob was totally caught off guard, and he was smiling from ear to ear. I had one birthday treat left for Rob and his son.

I was familiar with the vice president's schedule that day, and I timed our departure from the White House mess exactly right, so that we were exiting the West Wing at the same time the vice president was exiting to leave to an event off-site. I introduced Rob to the vice president, and the vice president wished him a happy birthday. What happened next was not planned but was typical Biden. Fran, who was always prepared and seemed to always know what Joe Biden was going to want and need, handed the VP a football. The vice president and Rob Lowe began to throw the football back and forth in the driveway.

Once the gridiron antics were completed, I thought Rob and his son would enjoy seeing the ceremonial office and the desk signed by so many vice presidents. As we climbed the dozens of majestic steps into the Eisenhower Executive Office Building that are lined by two enormous black anchors, I saw a female colleague come out the door at the top of the steps. We approached the top about the time that she was there, and when she realized it was Rob Lowe, she literally dropped her tray of lunch and a binder full of papers! Rob was so gracious in helping her pick up the papers and ensuring that she was not the least bit embarrassed. Too late—I was laughing and she was mortified!

If the Rob Lowe experience had occurred during my Clinton-Gore years, I don't think I would have possessed the maturity and wherewithal to have actually developed a meaningful friendship with someone like him. Fortunately, those Hollywood folks entered my life at a later stage, and Rob, like the Zuckers, is a friend to this day. As a matter of fact, as I was nearing the end of my tenure in the Biden office, I took a trip to Los Angeles.

From the minute I met Rob, he has always been warm, sincere, genuine, and completely approachable. I've dined with him and hung with him, and I am convinced that he has no clue that he is drop-dead gorgeous, famous and desired by every teenage girl, housewife and gay man in America, and maybe even some straight dudes! During that trip to Los Angeles, Rob so kindly invited me to be his guest on the set of the hit television show he was starring in at the time. I was a huge fan of *Brothers and Sisters*, so I was enthralled.

I would have been content to sit in a rickety old chair behind cameras and lights and just watch, but Rob made it an experience I would never forget. I arrived on the ABC lot to be driven in a golf cart to the *Brothers and Sisters* set. I entered the building and was instructed to go to the second or third floor, I don't recall, and find the door that said "Rob Lowe." Mr. Lowe would be waiting for me, as he had invited me to join him there for lunch. I found the door and knocked. It was all such an out-of-body experience for this guy who dreamed of being a performer but had shelved that creative dream for 20 years. All I heard was "Moe, is that you? Come on in." I opened the door only to find Rob shirtless and talking to his assistant about his schedule and to-do list. He hugged me, and I thought I had died and gone to heaven. A topless Rob Lowe hugging me... Do I need to write any more? He eventually put on a shirt, and our salads arrived. We engaged in one of our usual conversations about politics, Hollywood, the mutual admiration between Washington, D.C. and Hollywood and much more.

We finished our lunch, and Rob just kept making the experience more and more unforgettable. He said, "Come on, it's time for make-up." The next thing I know I'm sitting in an empty barber chair in a room full of mirrors. My "I don't get star struck around anyone" bullshit was about to be tested yet again when I realized that Sally Field, who played the maternal role on the show, was in the chair next to me. By the time make-up was done, Sally and Rob and I had laughed, debated and bonded.

I quickly followed them onto the set. Rob was to do a scene lying in a bed with his TV wife, Calista Flockhart. I have truly never seen anything like this before. Rob was standing with me and several of the cast and crew off set. We were carrying on a conversation about a variety of topics. The director of this particular episode simply called, "Ready," and Rob literally entered a makeshift door and got into the bed and into character and flawlessly shot a scene. I was in awe. The guy is so talented and experienced that he can go from Rob, my friend, to his character within minutes if not seconds and not miss a word or beat. Truly unbelievable.

In between Hollywood celebrity tours and hosting family and friends in the White House mess, I had the privilege of attending state arrivals on the South Lawn, White House events and numerous memorable evenings at the Naval Observatory with the Bidens—all the while fulfilling my duties as the director of management and administration, approving all expenses, doing budget projections and requests for the following fiscal year and interfacing with the White House office of administration on all technology and administrative matters, as well as coordinating with the Senate administrative office.

All the while keeping Ron fully informed and ensuring that our entire staff had the resources they needed to effectively serve the vice president, Dr. Biden and our nation. One of the challenges of working the endless hours that are required at the White House is trying to find a healthy work-life balance. I can't describe how many times over both tenures that I saw people succumb to physical illness and mental fatigue because of the strenuous demands on them. The second time I knew better.

During my Gore days, I found myself on four daily pills for stomach-related issues. My gastroenterologist conducted numerous endoscopies and colonoscopies on me and concluded each time that my "irritable bowel syndrome" and "nervous stomach" were a result of the stressful job and its demands. When I moved to Birmingham, AL, it was an ENT there who thought of checking me for food allergies. Once we discovered my severe gluten allergy, I never took another pill again. Regardless, I knew it was important to keep myself healthy and stay on top of my check-ups. I was fast approaching 50 years of age when I served with the Bidens. When I lived in Birmingham, AL, they discovered that I suffered from episodic atrial fibrillation due to a sporadic and momentary electrical malfunction between my brain and my heart, so it was time for my annual heart exam. Like millions of people, I had to do the stress test (a perfect reminder of how out of shape I am), and this time they also did a nuclear stress test. They injected me with the contrasting dye, and I was pleased that they determined that my heart was healthy and that of someone much younger. I was surprised, I must admit, because I was certain that the years of my addiction to bacon, pecan pie a la mode and countless other desserts had undoubtedly played havoc with my heart. I was relieved.

Employment at the White House means you don't take the entire day when you have your heart stress test. You actually get the test done as early in the day as possible so that you can hurry back to 1600 Pennsylvania Avenue and get back to work. I did exactly that. I decided that day to enter on the Pennsylvania Avenue entrance, where only staff can enter. As most people know, the section of Pennsylvania Avenue in front of the White House has been blocked off to vehicular traffic for many years as a result of 9/11. As I arrived at the Secret Service hut to pass through the magnetometers, I placed my backpack on the conveyer like normal and walked through the machine. Much to my surprise and that of the agents, the mag didn't go off, but the censor that detects radioactive material went off. I was oblivious that the nuclear stress test had made me radioactive. I was not allowed into the White House and had to call my cardiologist so he could explain to the agents, but that was not enough. They had to retrieve a device they use to measure the levels of radioactivity that my body was emitting and test my body. I felt like a living science experiment, but I was ultimately determined clear to go to work, but not until after a little embarrassment and anxiety.

I think one of the other aspects of coming back a second time with more maturity and wisdom that I enjoyed the most was the ability to keep things in perspective. I was older and was able to appreciate the magnitude of the role I played and enjoy it a manner I could not do the first time around. I took my job and role just as seriously, but I was able to live in the moment. Part of that comfort involved having a different kind of fun the second time. I was a peer and an equal, not only in age, but in responsibility, so it resulted in a different perspective of the experience. I was much more comfortable in my skin and stature this time, and it allowed me to relax.

By the time I returned to serve the Bidens, I had been a confidently open gay man for over 20 years, so the only use I had for a closet was to hold the clothes I had possessed for about that long. I was not going to change anything about my lifestyle or personal habits. In that spirit, the DNC gay and lesbian coordinator called me one day and asked if I would attend "drag bingo" at a popular gay bar in Washington, D.C., since it was going to be a fundraiser for the DNC. I, of course, was more than willing to attend and do my part by buying several bingo playing cards.

The room was filled with wonderful gay men and a smattering of lesbians. The drag queens were fun and entertaining and called some fierce games of bingo. To this day, I still can't believe it, but I think I won five of the eight games played that night, and each time I would go to the front and be given a gift for winning—gift certificates to local restaurants, T-shirts and the like. By the time I won the blackout final game, I could hear murmurs of, "That bitch, how does she keep winning." I was a good sport and went up to collect my fifth prize. The grand finale prize was four gay pornographic DVD's The titles were what you could imagine. I actually gave away two of them on my way back to my

seat to try and lessen the jealousy and ugly names they were calling me, and I placed the remaining two DVD's in my briefcase so
I could take them home and give them away as gag gifts later in
the year. (Wink! Wink!)

The next morning, I dressed for work like any normal day,
drove the eight miles to the Shady Grove metro stop and took
the red line in to the White House for another day of adventures
and history. It had become my routine to enter the Eisenhower-
executive office building through one of the center gates on 17th
Street. They tended to assign the same rotation of Secret Service
agents to the same gates, so you would become quite familiar
with them over time, and even know them by name and they
you.

On this particular morning, the two agents wished me a good
morning, and I wished them the same. I placed my briefcase on
the conveyor, and I walked through the mag. When I got to the
other side, the agent said he needed to hand check my bag. I was
taken aback, as I could not recall a time when that had occurred.
I, of course, complied. As he started emptying my bag, I'm not
sure how I did not faint on the spot when I saw him with a gay
pornographic DVD in each of his hands. The look on that poor
man's face was priceless, and the look on mine must have been
even more memorable. All I could think of saying was, "Those
aren't mine, I promise." The fact that they were in my bag was a
fact I seemed to overlook.

I think I went to every colleague's office and gave them something to laugh about for days. It was a story so few will ever be
able to tell, and sometimes I wonder if that craziness could only

happen to me. The levity and vulnerability that it allowed me to share bonded me even more with my colleagues. I firmly believe that it is stories like those that create equality and a connectedness that can only come when we share our vulnerability and humanity. I was not going to suffer alone through that memorable incident.

I'm not sure to this day why I selected Cathy Russell, Dr. Biden's chief of staff, but I know I had narrowed it down to her and Cynthia Hogan, our general counsel. I had ruled out playing a joke on Ron Klain because I wasn't quite ready to lose my job, although I know Ron has a good sense of humor and would have handled it perfectly, like he does everything he does in life. I made my way around our entire floor of vice presidential staff offices—Jay Carney couldn't stop laughing, and Evan Ryan, Pete Selfridge, Frank DiGiammarino, Cameron Moody, Jillian Doody, Zach Klein and so many more thought it was hilarious.

I finally arrived in Dr. Biden's suite of offices and noticed that Cathy Russell was not in her office nor at her desk. I made my way in there and saw her purse lying on the floor next to her desk. I loved Cathy, with her warm smile and wit She is a brilliant woman with an understated elegance. She is somewhat shy, but once you get to know her, she is so much fun to be around. I placed the two gay pornographic DVD'sin Cathy's open purse. I returned to my office halfway across the building. At about 3:00 p.m. that afternoon, I got a call on my cell phone, and the name on the screen displayed Cathy Russell. She was howling, and I could picture how she turns a little red when she gets embarrassed. She just kept saying, "I'm going to get you" and "I can't believe you did that." I actually sat at the Wilmington train station with Cathy and her husband, Tom Donilon, President Obama's former national security advisor, after Beau Biden's funeral and, five years later, Cathy still turned red and howled with laughter as we remembered that funny day.

I want to make clear that a senior role in the White House comes with an enormous responsibility and high-risk consequences. You can't let up for one second, and you are reminded each minute of each day of each week of the year that your actions, words or lack of attention could embarrass not only yourself, the president and the vice president, but our nation as well. The flights on Air Force Two and all the historic events were like a mini reward for all the sacrifices and long hours that were expected and required.

One of the highlights of my Biden tenure and, frankly, my life, was the announcement of the appointment of the first Hispanic to the United States Supreme Court. Fortuitously, Vice President Biden had served as chairman of the Judiciary Committee in the United States Senate for several years. His leadership role was highlighted during the Clarence Thomas hearings due to the shocking allegations and testimony from Anita Hill.

Vice President Biden continues to be viewed as one of our nation's experts on Supreme Court nominations, and several of his senior staff from the Senate Judiciary Committee were now my colleagues in the White House. When President Obama made his visionary appointment of the fierce and wise Latina, Judge Sonia Sotomayor of New York, the president's staff turned to the vice president and my colleagues to spearhead the preparation proceedings for Judge Sotomayor.

This was one of the most fateful days of my journey so far, because the president selected Cynthia Hogan—the former counsel at the Senate Judiciary Committee under Vice President Biden and now his general counsel—as head of the prep team alongside the traditional folks from the White House counsel's office, like my dear friend the late Cassandra Butts. Cynthia and me had become very close friends and worked inextricably together on all budget, operations and administrative matters. She is a highly skilled attorney with an uncanny ability to prevent missteps and errors.

Lucky for me, Cynthia's office was adjacent to mine. The first day of Judge Sotomayor's prep was held in Cynthia's office. Unbeknownst to me, there was a group of staff meeting with the Judge around noon that day. All of a sudden, in my office door walks Cynthia Hogan and Sonia Sotomayor. At that moment in time, I didn't care that I thought they were handing Justice Sotomayor to me because I was the highest-ranking Hispanic in the vice president's office. The reason could have been because I wear glasses or I'm chubby and bald—I was thrilled that I got to spend time with a woman I admired greatly. Cynthia suggested that I take Justice Sotomayor to lunch so she could get a break from the intensity of the preparation meetings.

One of the most remarkable women in the world—
Justice Sonia Sotomayor

I know in my heart that the real reason Cynthia brought Sonia and me together was because she knew we would become fast friends, and my heritage and culture had nothing at all to do with it. Justice Sotomayor and I went to lunch that day, and the next, and many more after that. On some days, I would host her mother for lunch, as she had accompanied her daughter to the White House to some of those prep sessions.. Over this incredible period of time, Justice Sotomayor and I engaged in personal conversations, and it gave me the blessed opportunity to get to know a remarkable woman and jurist.

In my personal and professional interactions with Justice Sotomayor, I found her to be extraordinarily humble and approachable. I also found her to possess a quiet confidence, and her success and accomplishments never seemed to cloud the memories of where she came from in the projects of the Bronx, her tumultuous childhood and her responsibility and commitment to Hispanics. It was apparent from the minute I met this inspirational lady that she was intelligent and wise, not just from a legal and scholarly perspective, but about life. Thanks to Cynthia, I was allowed to attend the historic proceedings that were her confirmation hearings. I silently wept, as I knew I was witnessing the manifestation of the toil and labor of our ancestors before us, including my uncle who had been one of our nation's first Hispanic federal judges.

The following Halloween after her confirmation to the Supreme Court, Justice Sotomayor was still the talk of the country. She had graced the cover of every major newspaper and magazine worth reading. I decided that it would be fitting to dress as Justice Sonia Sotomayor for Halloween. I actually received a standing ovation at a bar that Halloween night. At a reception honoring my and Justice Sotomayor's mutual and close friend, Mari Carmen Aponte, for her appointment as ambassador to El Salvador, I mustered up the courage to show Justice Sotomayor a picture of me as her! What do they say—imitation is the greatest form of flattery? It is my understanding that picture of me as her remains on her cell phone to this day.

Last fall, she so graciously and lovingly officiated at the wedding of my special friends, Ingrid Duran and Catherine Pino. There was an electricity in the room because of the love everyone has for Catherine and Ingrid, and a celebratory air accompanied the electricity and love because of the mere historic aspect of marriage equality, with a Supreme Court Justice present to officiate. Justice Sotomayor spoke so eloquently and emotionally of her dear friends, Catherine and Ingrid, but not before she walked down the aisle, saw me and stopped to hug and kiss me and tell me that she still had the Halloween picture on her phone. I, like millions of others, love Justice Sotomayor. I consider it one of the greatest privileges of my life to call her a mentor, shero and friend.

I got a standing ovation at a Halloween party as Sonia Sotomayor

Politics and public service are honorable and worthy professions. I have seen the best of each and the worst. It is not for the thin-skinned nor faint of heart. Through the political and public service arena, I made some of the closest friends any man would be fortunate to have, and I was exposed to information and experiences that have shaped and impacted me. I learned more than these pages could ever reflect. And I am proud to say that the positive and the good I experienced in my two White House tenures far outweighed the negative.

The Bidens--I cherish my time of service to them and proud to call them friends.

CHAPTER FIFTEEN

I WILL NEVER FULLY UNDERSTAND NOR COMPREHEND HOW ONE child in the world is born into poverty and famine and another born into wealth and privilege. I refuse to engage in any semblance of blind faith so that I can feel some sort of peace about not knowing the answers to many questions in life.

I do know that I am incredibly fortunate to have been born into the Vela and Yanez families—not for any materialistic nor superficial reason, but because of the love for family, respect for community and spirit of service that was passed down for generations AND because I was born into one of the most awesome cultures in the world.

I love being Hispanic/Latino. I love our culture and zest for life. I love the passion that runs in our blood. I love the emotion with which we experience the journey of life. The cultural traditions and practices have brought me comfort, security and warmth during troubled times. Our culture is a glass half full type of culture, and finding the positive is a way of life. Being Hispanic means being grateful—grateful for the chance to be on this planet no matter what one's circumstances.

It has been my Hispanic culture and heritage that has been an integral part of my core. I firmly believe that it is from there that I receive my compassion for those less fortunate, my passion, my celebratory nature and my abiding love for others and life.

As with all other things in life, the good is most likely accompanied by shortfalls. I will be criticized by many in our community for being so open, transparent and honest about our community's greatest problems, but we will never grow, learn and evolve if we can't acknowledge our weaknesses.

We suffer from a serious flaw that I liken to a pendemic disease in the Latino community, and it is not healthcare related. There are sociological theories and philosophies about this horrific pattern, and it plagues our community and stifles our growth and empowerment. For years, our community has wondered privately why we can't seem to gain traction or power on a national level from a political, economic and social perspective. There are many reasons why this reality remains elusive, but I am confident in saying that a major reason is this pattern of obstructionism demonstrated between Hispanics.

Some refer to this as a sociological theory called the "Crab Theory"—I just call it stupid, short-sighted and sad. When a Latino works tirelessly and achieves a level of success, whether it be through education, business or socio-economics, it's as if we are all crabs in a large barrel. Latinos climbing the social ladder of success is equivalent to crabs climbing up the sides of the barrel to reach the top and get out to what would represent success among the masses. Latinos (crabs) in the barrel who remain below will jump up, collude and collaborate to pull the hind claws of those climbing up to success until they come falling back down. I, like so many others in our community, have experienced first-hand the power of those claws pulling me down (recall the stories of the Democratic Convention and Obama colleagues).

Clearly, I am not a sociologist nor psychologist, and so I can only surmise and speculate as to why so many in our community choose to live their lives with this level of animosity, jealousy and spite. We are a culture of positive energy and good will, and this flies in the face of our traditional cultural values.

I am convinced after many years of observing, experiencing and studying this phenomenon that it is rooted in some sort of severe insecurity. I think the history of Hispanics in the United States, in general, is primarily migratory and a prime example of people coming to this nation to achieve the American dream. For some reason, there remains in our community a deep-rooted fear that if one in our community rises, it will leave the others behind. I can only imagine that this act of prevention and obstruction is a result of jealousy and insecurity—plain and simple.

The irony is that achieving economic power, political clout and full equality will require us to achieve economic parity. In order to achieve this economic parity, we must genuinely be supportive of one another, encourage each other's growth and advocate for each member of our community to reach their God-given potential. Then and only then will we have an equal seat at the table that will be truly reflective of the 55 million-plus consumers and citizens we currently represent in the U.S. population. We will be the majority of this nation in the next several decades, so time is of the essence for us to understand the need to act cohesively and in a mutually beneficial manner.

In every speech I give to Latino audiences, I use the example that has been the most evident to me that represents my solution to our internal obstructionism. I reference the Jewish community. As I shared earlier, I have worked side by side with many of my Jewish brothers and sisters in politics, public service, business, charitable organizations and activist causes. I am not suggesting they are without their own internal community challenges, and they will admit to that, but they are a prime example of internal community cohesion and loyalty.

They might not always agree with one another, but when it comes to supporting one another, they are there for one another, driven by a sense of community. It is amazing and inspirational how Jews support one another, particularly in business endeavors. I often say that if a customer comes into a jewelry shop and asks for a pear-shaped diamond of three carats set in a certain way and Mr. Lowenstein does not have it, he will draw the customer a map on how to get to Mr. Feldman's store two blocks away. If you go to Mr. Gonzales's bodega and he does not carry what you seek, you are shit out of luck—he will not send you to Mr. Sanchez!

We must learn from the cohesion and supportive nature of the Jewish community.

From a sociological perspective, it is quite interesting that the Jewish community does not play the "victim" card, nor does one feel they have a sense of entitlement. Yet the Jews have been exiled and decimated, and to this day there are those who want to extinguish their existence. Rather than whine, complain and dwell on their victimization, they realized that economic success, unification as a people and upward mobility of even the less fortunate among them is vital to thrive and achieve.

I humbly suggest that not only the Latino community can learn from this example, but other cultures and communities as well. We don't forget the past, but at some point, true freedom and equality will only be achieved when we are not hostage to the past. I believe that we as Latinos are too busy thinking individually instead of raising one another up and truly acting like a community.

Again, I am proud to be of Mexican heritage. I love being a Latino and I will do my part until my dying breath to help our community reach parity on every stage and in every forum. As I have become quite adept at business development, marketing, public relations and communications, I have come to the conclusion and I have observed with much grief and frustration that today in America, we Hispanics have a severe branding deficiency.

Much like a product or company must build a brand that is trustworthy, respected, desired and valued, we as a Latino community must do exactly the same. In addition to our internal community obstructionism, we suffer from a profound misperception of who we are today in the United States. We are not monolithic, yet people make us out to be. We have more in common between Mexicans, Puerto Ricans, Cubans, Dominicans, Central Americans, Spaniardsand South Americans than we do different, but what is different among us is rich in culture and tradition. We all eat tamales, but they might be made differently or with a unique texture, wrapping or consistency. We all love Latin music, but it might be nuanced as mariachi, salsa, merengue, rumba, flamenco or tango.

Our branding challenges are a result of our rapidly powerful consumer buying power. As our buying power has grown, American and global companies are desperately trying to ensure that their products and services are consumed by our community. We are the largest ethnic minority in the country and will one day be the majority of this nation. If they don't figure it out now, they will be playing catch up for years to come and be left at the station. It's not as easy as it sounds. There is no silver bullet because of the rich diversity within our community.

Plain and simply put,- the Hispanic community needs to rebrand itself. For far too long, non-Hispanics across our nation have viewed us only as those who landscape their yards, clean their hotel rooms ,wash the dishes and cook the food at restaurants. We are far more than that. With all due respect to Cesar Chavez and President Obama, their slogan of "Sí Se Puede" (Yes We Can) has outlived its effectiveness. That slogan is no longer a true representation of today's U.S. Latino population and contributions to society. If we continue to say, "Yes we can," then it implies that we have not yet. That is the farthest thing from the truth.

Part of our rebranding and message to our nation must be "Ya Somos" (We Are). We are making a difference in ways that impact the lives of all Americans each and every day—we are astronauts, doctors, lawyers, university chancellors, cancer researchers, chemists, members of Congress, preachers, teachers, professors, electricians and plumbers and are in every profession, sector and industry known to man. And, yes, we landscape yards, wash dishes, cook and clean hotel rooms with an incomparable work ethic and second to none.

We are proud of the legends like Cesar Chavez, Dolores Huerta, Corky Gonzalez, Willie Velasquez, Raul Yzaguirre and countless others who paved the path, but it is time to highlight the new Latino entrepreneurs, innovators, inventors and technologists who are developing new and cutting-edge ways to simplify and empower our lives. We are so much more than a few national non-profits, and we are more than the same faces and people who are paraded out as representatives of our community time and time again. We are worth investing in as a consumer base. We are the largest ethnic minority in the United States. We are deeply loyal, hard-working, faithful and ambitious. We are visionary. We are loving, kind and compassionate, and we are passionate, above all. We are not combative and don't play the victim nor race card at every turn. We are here, we are equal, we are contributing in major ways to the fabric of our society, and we are going nowhere.

The promise of the future looks very bright for the Latino community. These last several years, I have had the chance to befriend and mentor several Latino Millennials. Sergio Gonzales, Sam Jammal, Daniel Suvor, Jennifer Molina, Fatima Orozco Rojas, Jose Aristimuno, Ximena Gonzales and countless others are incredible examples of why we should invest in the next generation of Latino leaders. Sergio was the youngest deputy chief of staff of any federal agency, as he dutifully served Director

Katherine Archuleta at the office of personnel management. Ximena is from my home area, and she has served as deputy social secretary to the president and Mrs. Obama at the White House and deputy chief of staff in the office of presidential personnel. We have thousands of young Latino leaders like them across this great nation: Alida Garcia, Andrea Pacheco Dhamer, Kenneth Sandoval, Laura Castillo and thousands of others. We must nurture, guide, encourage, support and love them. They are truly the future of our nation.

CHAPTER SIXTEEN

I CAN SAY WITHOUT ANY RESERVATION OR RETICENCE THAT being gay was the greatest gift the universe ever gave me. For all the struggles in the coming out process and the incredible challenges that accompanied the reconciliation of my gayness with my culture and religious upbringing, it has allowed me to see life through a different prism. I love the view!

Once I reached that level of self-confidence, self-worth and peace that is required to experience freedom, being gay has provided me with a perspective that has, I hope, made me more compassionate, less judgmental and definitely more inclusive. I am convinced that my ability to love freely and often is a result of being gay. I don't want to in any way take away from the valuable and powerful lessons I was taught by my parents, but being gay has fueled my passion and my soul.

Oftentimes I sit and ponder about how I can still feel so positive and grateful to be gay when, in reality, many in the gay community have caused me severe damage. I am not alone in this regard; gay men can be cruel and cliquish through words and actions. For over 30 years, I have never truly felt accepted nor respected by the gay community. I have battled with weight issues for most of my adult life. In the gay community, the societal emphasis and standards of beauty are heightened. The focus on the external, such as hair, body structure, appearance, skin care and fashion are standards on which gays tend to place an even higher level of importance and reliance when it comes to acceptance. I have never been able to meet those standards and, although I have reached a certain level of success in my career and have become a confident man, in my rawest form, it hurts.

For many years, this feeling of rejection in the community kept me from participating in gay causes or frequenting gay bars. Anyone who has felt the sting of being stigmatized as not skinny enough or pretty enough will tell you that it never quite leaves your psyche. I hope by sharing this profoundly intimate account, just a few more gay men will gain a newfound awareness and sensitivity to the value of inclusion and basic human dignity.

There is probably a myriad of reasons why the LGBT community places such an extraordinary premium on the external and superficial, but I will always hold out hope that one by one we will all come to realize that each person is worthy and that beauty is ultimately found in one's soul. As a single gay man at the writing of this book, it is overwhelming how many times a chubby gay man will hear, "You are awesome but you are just not my "type"—code for, "You are too fat, too skinny, not beautiful enough, too bald, too this or too that."

I realized that I have two choices in life. One is to allow others to determine my happiness and define who I am OR the other is to recognize that I am not on this earth to meet the standards or expectations of others—I am only here to live up to my own standards and expectations. I have set those standards high, and I prefer to live, laugh and love as I strive to achieve them. If someone chooses not to love me in return, frankly, it is their loss. They will never get to experience the warmth of my embrace nor the comfort of my love.

I decided long ago that this journey is short and my time on this Earth is limited, if you keep it in perspective. I only get one shot at this and I will not allow the insecurities of those around me to determine my feelings or emotions nor fuel my own insecurities. They cannot and will not have that power over me. Only I possess that power.

I am fortunate that my dear friend, Tony Varona, the associate dean at the Washington College of Law, invited me to lunch about five years ago. Like me, Tony is a Hispanic gay professional and attorney, far more brilliant and talented than I ever will be. Over that lunch, Tony asked me what my bucket list might look like, as I had just completed my second tenure in the White House. No one had asked me that question before, so I was taken aback, since an answer was not readily available in my mind nor heart. I gave it some thought and responded by telling Tony that I felt like the Rodney Dangerfield of the Hispanic and gay communities. Like Rodney Dangerfield, I didn't feel like I got any respect! I explained to my friend that maybe if I had the chance to teach on the collegiate or post-graduate level that it might help me overcome those insecurities and garner some of the respect that had eluded me.

Tony changed my life in two major ways at that moment in time. As the academic dean at the law school, he wasted no time in assuring me that he would create a class for me to teach to second and third year law students that would combine my legal education with my extensive political and government experience. I have since taught the class at least two semesters, and I found it to be one of the most rewarding and meaningful experiences of my life. For a split second in those classrooms, I actually believed it when they called me Professor Vela!

Tony is actually one of the most intelligent and intellectual people I've ever met, and I had watched him teach his first year contracts class and knew that he was a natural. I will never forget the preparation meeting with Tony the month before I taught my first class. I was actually nervous (and that is rare) and greatly intimidated (and that is rare) at the thought that my students could very well be smarter than me. Tony so graciously agreed to give me some pointers and helpful hints. I arrived in Tony's office with a former colleague that was to co-teach with me only to find a stack of about 15 to 20 books that started on the floor and rose to eye level as we sat at the table. This was my worst nightmare, and I was sure that I had bitten off more than I could chew. I was in way over my head. Not only had Tony prepared as if this was a dissertation, but he actually had yellow sticky notes in strategic places in every single one of those books of matters he wanted to discuss with us. I literally felt the blood leave my head and my heart palpitate. For anyone who knows me, if it's not in *People* magazine, then I probably have not read it!

I listened and took meticulous notes, and the first day of class arrived in what felt like a flash. I had almost 30 2L and 3L, and a couple of LLM students as well. From the first minute, I knew they would impact my life in ways I had never imagined. I reviewed my notes from Tony and was relieved to find out the first class was a softball, because it involved mostly organizational and introductory matte.s. As Tony had suggested, I started in the front row and asked them to share their name, hometown, undergraduate university, why they were in law school, what they wanted to get out of our class and my co-professor suggested we ask what literary work had most impacted their life as a good ice breaker. I knew I should not have listened to my colleagueon that last one.

I loved connecting with my students on their team mascots from the schools they had attended, football references and anecdotes on the many cities they represented. However, asking their literary work was the worst mistake I have ever made. Each one of these gifted and talented future leaders and lawyers was rattling off some *New York Times* bestseller or classic novel. I had not read even one of them, so I was growing pale and feeling quite inadequate by the time we got to the sixteenth student. Finally, the sixteenth student announced that his favorite literary work was *Running with Scissors* by Augusten Burroughs—a gay author with gay-centric content. I think I let out a primal scream of joy. It was a momentary feeling of adequacy, and the literary work pronouncement by the twenty-eighth student could not come soon enough.

I'm proud to say that I survived that first semester, and Tony went on to read my student reviews and critiques at several functions since then—I was humbled and touched by the kind comments of so many of them. Maybe someday they will realize that I received much more from them than they did from me. Thanks to Tony, I now know that even I can be a law school professor, and now only swimming naked with someone I love in a lagoon under the moonlight in Tahiti is the only thing that remains on my bucket list!

The second incredible way that Tony impacted my life at that delightful lunch was by asking me if I would consider being on the national board of GLAAD. GLAAD is the Gay and Lesbian Alliance Against Defamation. They are highly respected and valued as the watchdog of mainstream media and commentary as it pertains to words, actions and attitudes toward the LGBT community. I had always admired their ability to call out major corporations and the media when they inadvertently or intentionally projected the LGBT community in anything less than a positive light. I was humbled that he thought I could contribute to this incredible organization's mission. He asked, I accepted and the GLAAD board approved. As with almost everything I do in life, I became passionately involved. I met some very talented LGBT leaders and allies as well. It was truly the first time on my journey that I felt respected and welcomed within the LGBT community. It was rewarding, but not without the drama (extra because it was a gay organization), human dynamics and power plays that are associated with most organizations. Overall, it was a very rewarding experience and a personal breakthrough for me.

Like almost every gay or lesbian I know, coming out to one's parents is by far the most traumatizing and harrowing experience of the process. After hearing hundreds of individual stories so far, I count my blessings to have the parents I have. By no stretch of the imagination was it easy, but somehow deep inside, I knew there was absolutely no way they would stop loving me. Both of my parents received the information with an immediate affirmation of their love for me but with a multitude of questions that one would expect in a situation like that.

In hindsight, my greatest fear was not of rejection from my parents, but at the thought that my siblings would one day not let me be around their children. It is unbelievable how fear and anxiety can make someone almost paranoid and how our minds play games with us. As I mentioned earlier, my siblings would no more keep me from their children than the sun stay away from the earth. My fears and trepidation were unfounded; I have the ten most amazing nephews and nieces, and I'm the proudest uncle in the world.

As a man who has been openly gay for 30 years now, I have also observed with tremendous sadness the swath of destruction that is the result of drugs and alcohol in the gay community. I may be wrong, but there appears to be a disproportionate amount of drug and alcohol abuse in our community, and I have often wondered why. I surmise that it must be the result of a myriad of underlying causes—some self-loathing and the misconception that you need drugs and alcohol to have fun, but I believe that the primary cause is a profound need to escape from the reality of being gay. I purport that this escapism that manifests itself through alcohol and drug abuse occurs when a person is not prepared to fully accept and love themselves for who they are. After a rough start in this complex process of accepting and loving one's self, as they say in Hollywood, I'm in a good place and am a living testimony that alcohol and drugs are not necessary to reach this peaceful place.

We each have insecurities, and trying to hide them or pretending that they don't exist is what I believe gets us in trouble.

I find that confronting your insecurities, owning them and, most importantly, understanding them so you can overcome them is the truest foundation for peace and a path to self-acceptance. I don't think we can take our foot off the gas pedal, as we are complex as human beings, and we have layers upon layers of insecurities and flaws that are a result of past experiences and hurts.

As difficult and scary as it is to analyze and assess one's own past actions and behavior patterns, it has been the greatest source of strength for me in growing and evolving. As I reflect on my two past failed romantic relationships, it has become apparent to me that I fell prey to those pesky and annoying insecurities.

It is blatantly clear that my tendency to be in control in a relationship and of the situations surrounding those relationships is a direct manifestation of those anxiety-ridden days when my mom was dropping off my lonely island self in the middle of the sea. As an adult, my insecurity is rooted in the fear of people leaving me and being alone again, so I have traditionally been demanding and controlling in a romantic relationship. I recognize that admitting this may keep me from getting a husband, but the good news is that I have learned to confront that demon. I work on it every day of my life. I have stared this insecurity in the face, and I am winning the battle.

I am comfortable with being alone for the first time in my life, and I'm at peace with the concept that I may not find love again. I had two chances at it and, like so many others, my insecurities succeeded in damaging what could have been a healthy and everlasting love. I don't want to be too harsh on myself, because both of my partners had their own share of issues that contributed to the demise of the relationships. But I can only be responsible for me, my actions and my shortcomings. After all is said and done, I am committed to the premise that I'd rather be single than settle.

I have learned from those disappointments. I have learned that I have to believe in myself. I know that if I love myself and truly ask myself constantly why I say what I say and why I do what I do, I will continue evolving as a human being. I am also cognizant that you get back what you put out—I find that if I smile, love and laugh with even strangers, nine times out of ten, I get love, a smile and laughter in return. I will take that return on investment all the time.

I have also experienced those grumpy, bitter and negative souls who don't have the courage to confront their demons and who just go through life on the miserable surface. I avoid them like the plague, and if my path has to cross theirs, I know that I get to determine how they affect me; solely I can determine what my reaction will be. I choose to be positive and optimistic. Who knows—they might even see something they like in my disposition and others who share it. I have to constantly fight the urge to judge others when they don't share my bubbly and hopeful outlook on life, but I quickly remind myself that we truly don't know another person's situation nor station in life. Their situation may be dire, and far be it for me to speculate or criticize. You know, walk in those moccasins...

As I get older, I grow less patient when it comes to those who choose to skate on the surface of life. Yes, it's easier, safer and more comfortable for most, but it also is the least rewarding. I choose depth and quality; it might mean less in quantity, but I will take quality over quantity all day long.

I am opinionated and headstrong at times, and I own that. Combining those traits with my gaytino passion, it can be quite an adventure to debate me, I suspect. It's a combination that can get me in trouble, but I have come to the conclusion that if I stick to facts and the truth, then I don't mind alienating a few folks along the way. Much like my foray to Broadway right after undergraduate school, I live my life trying never to regret any of my actions or relationships.

I have no regrets so far in life except for not having children. I believe in my heart that I would have been a great dad—coaching Little League football and baseball, braiding my daughter's hair or attending dance and piano recitals. I don't even regret either of my two failed romantic relationships. I wish they had been lifelong, but I have learned, evolved and grown immensely from both of them. In my 13-year relationship with Deiv, we traveled the world, made unforgettable memories and had a beautiful life.

Similarly, I don't regret my second, four-year relationship with a man named Brian. He was a dashing young man who heard me give a speech from the back of a cavernous ballroom and pursued me on Facebook. The fact that he lived on the west coast and was almost 25 years younger than me gave me serious pause but his charm, ambition and spirit won me over. Within two months, Brian moved across the country to be with me and begin what resulted in four years of laughter, incredible travels, some amazing memories and many rocky and tumultuous times as well. Our relationship was never quite healthy, although it had tremendous potential. Once again, the fact that most of us gays never had the luxury of learning how to date like our heterosexual brethren can have catastrophic consequences when you merge two individuals without taking the time to truly get to know one another and set the proper foundation for meaningful growth and connection.

I learned some serious life lessons from that most recent relationship. I look back and realize that everything that happens on our journey happens for a reason. I was supposed to learn that age is not the barrier to love, but rather, that in order for a relationship to be healthy and productive, both parties must be mentally, emotionally, spiritually and physically available at the same moment on their respective journeys. Both Brian and I brought baggage, demons and insecurities into the relationship and, in the end, they destroyed something very special. My connection with and love for Brian was profound and deep, though not always understood by some. Against many odds, we had four beautiful years together and I miss his presence in my life, but cherish the memories.

I also learned the hard way that it is vital to the success of a relationship that neither party ever lose their individuality and independence—it is imperative that each of us continue to grow as a person so that we are that much more equipped to contribute to the growth of us as a couple. When it comes to relationships, sometimes I wish there was a mulligan, like in golf—if I knew then what I know now!

After is all said and done, I am a hopeless romantic, as is the Latin tradition. My Latino passion and heart full of love will always be ready in case the universe blesses me with another chance. I am more prepared and equipped than I have ever been, but I have also found the elusive peace that I have been seeking for most of my journey. I no longer yearn for nor need a partner to be at peace, but I welcome a partner with which to share the journey. The only thing I know is that they will be loved, respected and celebrated and meet an improving and evolving Moe Vela.

CHAPTER SEVENTEEN

ONE OF THE MOST REWARDING RESULTS OF MY EXCITING journey thus far has been witnessing and being exposed to a variety of effective leadership styles. From community leaders and teachers to fellow entrepreneurs and two vice presidents of the United States, I have witnessed many leadership traits that work and some that are completely ineffective. Witnessing the various styles has been the foundation upon which to become a successful business development consultant and entrepreneur.

There are certainly common traits among the successful leaders in my life, and I would dare say the most important one was that they had earned the RESPECT of those they were leading. How they earned the respect might differ, but that respect was the foundation in their ability to lead. Sometimes, in the case of the two vice presidents or Ron Klain, for example, it was deep-rooted respect for the role they played in our nation and for their previous accomplishments. Those three gentlemen also earned respect through their demeanor, disposition and determination.

I have watched corporate and community leaders share another important trait, and that is the ability to build consensus.

My observation is that to build consensus, you have to demonstrate a genuine and sincere appreciation for the opinions, viewpoints and input of others, and you must seek such. I have seen this consensus-building exercise backfire and fail when it is blatantly a fake exercise and the so-called leader is simply going to do what they desire regardless of the input.

The leaders in my life have taught me so much. One of the most effective tools that I use as a leader that I learned from a few along the way is that of self-deprecation. By laughing at yourself, you are representing that you are equally vulnerable and equally flawed, and that we are in this together. I start every speech I deliver by saying, "It's such a pleasure for this chubby, gay, ugly Latino from south Texas to be here with you today!" From the onset, I have about 75% of the audience following me because they can relate to me. There is not a day that goes by that we each feel less than beautiful or a little pudgy in places or like an underdog—they are with me from that moment forward and will actually listen to my remarks. Let me point out that I don't particularly believe that I'm ugly (though I'm not Rob Lowe), but I am chubby, gay, bald and from South Texas! A word of caution—I gave this opening to a speech I delivered in London, Ontario and following my remarks, I noticed there was an extraordinarily long line of folks that wanted to hug me or take a picture with me. For a split second, I thought I might have delivered good remarks, but I quickly realized that my self-deprecation resulted in the Canadians wanting to assure me that I was indeed handsome, loveable and worthy! It backfired a little, but I still recommend the approach—I got lots of hugs and nice comments!

The most powerful leadership tool that I use and that I have found the most effective is that of humor. It is a proven fact that when we laugh, we feel good. I find that, as a leader, if I can make a person laugh, they are much more apt to follow, listen, adhere and participate. It has made being a leader a much more enjoyable and rewarding experience, because the laughter and shared humor are a bonding tool that result in a more successful collaboration.

Yet another leadership tool that has proven to be effective for me and for so many whose leadership I have witnessed first-hand is that of simply having FUN. Leaders who lose sight of the fact that we are more productive when we are enjoying an experience are less successful leaders, and it is manifested in a less productive team or a less than exemplary project.

In my many years of interacting and transacting with Fortune 500 CEOs and C-suite executives, as well as high-level government officials, I too often see their ultra-serious and intense approach to leadership. Many people disagree with me, but I am convinced that leaders who remain light-hearted, who don't take themselves too seriously and who know how to inject fun and good will into their business endeavors are the ones with the most rewarding experiences and with the most loyal followers.

Far too often, leaders allow their egos to get the best of them. In those meetings that I must frequent, inevitably, these private and public sector titans will begin to drop big acronyms, business lingo and references to articles and books they have read. It used to be horribly intimidating to me until I realized through experience that true leadership is not measured in how academic nor familiar we are with big words and lots of literature, but whether those around us respect, like, admire and trust us.

The very same holds true for business: At the end of the day, people still have to like you, trust you and respect you to buy your product or use your service. Business owners are more likely to align and team with other business owners they respect, admire, like and trust. Investors are more likely to invest in a great concept or business model when it's owned and managed by people they respect, admire, like and trust. In real estate it's about location, location, location. In life and business, it's about relationships, relationships, relationships and they must be real and meaningful.

In my current role as the owner of The Vela Group, a business development consulting firm, we have finally found a way to monetize relationships. Over the past 30 years of my career, I have been blessed to amass over 20,000 relationships in a diversity of sectors, geographies and walks of life. When I made the conscious decision to leverage and parlay that extensive network into a business, I made a commitment that it would be under one very strict condition with no exceptions. I take those relationships seriously, and the majority of them are people I admire, respect and even love. In order to reach out to them on behalf of my clients or for business enterprises, I insist that there must be mutual benefit. Both parties must have some gain from the interaction. Much like a marriage or any relationship, for it to be healthy and successful, there must be mutual gain. I also put into practice a life lesson that my parents taught us—to nurture and enhance relationships with a genuine heart and spirit. People know when you just care about them for simply business purposes—the nurturing and enhancing is best done when you DON'T need them, but simply care. At the end of the day, leveraging and parlaying relationships must not be or be perceived as abusive to the existing relationship.

I am fortunate to have mentored hundreds of young professionals and Millennials. I am often asked, "How do you make it to the White House twice, or how does one engage in a successful career like yours?" My initial response is one of gratitude for viewing my journey as a successful career, but I quickly pivot to destroy the notion that it is all about "networking." I believe that networking is a practice of the past.

Attending events and conferences and exchanging hundreds of business cards is just not enough anymore. I tell these brilliant young people that it is imperative that they build relationships that are based on genuine CONNECTION. Connection is not a text nor social media exchange nor even handing each other your business cards with a handshake. Connection is ensuring that when you meet that person at an event or conference, or on a plane or train, that you connect in a meaningful manner. You must stand out in their mind or their heart—whether it be through humor, confidence, humility, warmth, graciousness, approachability or love, you want them to remember you. Likewise, you know you have connected when you remember them and they remember YOU! That is not the end of the process but merely the beginning. The nurturing and enhancing are vital next steps.

I also remind these Millennials and young professionals that one must be flexible, adaptable and open to the unexpected opportunities the universe might bring them. If we remain too set in our ways, too rigid, too sure of ourselves, one never knows what you might have missed, passed up or ignored. In hindsight, I am eternally grateful that I had never pre-determined my path and let life take its course. My career, in the eyes of many, is a hodgepodge, but I can look back with no regrets and I can certainly see the reason for each of those amazing experiences.

Speaking of Millennials, one of my greatest frustrations in life has been the frequency with which I hear or see a Millennial suffering from what I call the "Zuckerberg syndrome." I admire Mark Zuckerberg immensely, and I post on Facebook almost daily, so I honor the fact that he has changed and impacted the world in incomparable ways. Fortunately for him, but unfortunately for the rest of us, the odds of becoming a billionaire by 30 years of age are so miniscule that one probably has a better chance of getting struck by lightning or hit by a car.

This and the other examples of technology stratospheric success have created a Millennial workforce, at least in my experience, that does not fully understand that we must pay our dues and work our way up the ladder of life. There will be those who skip dozens of rungs on that ladder like Mark Zuckerberg and the Google guys and others, but they are by far the exception to the rule.

Our Millennials are much more brilliant, prepared and equipped to lead the world than my generation is, but I encourage them to understand that wisdom is the result of life experience and that no new software or app or technology is going to ever replace life experience and the wisdom that comes from it.

Simply creating a new app does not leadership skills create—you learn those as you go along; you develop them; you earn them like your stripes.

The beauty of making mistakes and learning from them, as well as, having been fortunate to have been blessed with many rewarding,interesting, historic, successful and invigorating experiences in both the public and private sectors is that I can build upon those experiences and apply them in a diversity of ways in my future. I have watched, listened, observed and learned from so many and I get to put all of those lessons to good use as I now have less tomorrows then I do yesterdays, but I have every intention of making them count. My current intentions are to continue using The Vela Group as a way to help businesses to grow and reach their potential and to use my Vela Publishing and Motivational Press publishing partnership to give access to minority, women, LGBT and other authors who will educate, enlighten, motivate and inspire us. I will use my new production company, Telemoevela Productions to focus some of my energy on returning to my creative self and working on creative projects and endeavors that I put aside and shelved in order to experience what the universe has so generously provided me thus far. Who knows, you might yet see me on Broadway!!!!

CLOSING

I'VE HAD AN AMAZING JOURNEY SO FAR. IT'S NO DIFFERENT OR better than most. I don't view myself as special nor entitled. My journey is just mine—with its struggles, challenges, triumphs and joys. I've been fortunate to have a unique platform, perspective and point of view. My only hope is that somehow my story will inspire, motivate, unite and encourage others to live their truth—whatever it may be.

By any stretch of the imagination, I've had a great run so far. By materialistic and financial standards, I am not successful solely because of my inferior and pitiful money management skills. Howeer, I measure my good fortune and success by the amount of love that surrounds me. By that measurement standard, I'm filthy rich! My goal for the rest of my days on this incredible earth is to live them with an abiding and unending gratitude. I have met and grown to love and respect those who would credit their good fortune and goodness to their religious beliefs—Christians, Jews, Muslims, Hindus, Buddhists and others—I respect that. I realized awhile back, at least for me, that although I'm a gambling man, this is not a gamble I am willing to take. When you know and respect someone in each of those groups and they are each certain they are right about their beliefs and convictions, one quickly realizes that they can't all be right. It was a disappointing, frustrating and even frightening realization, but I am now at peace with not taking sides.

I'm a spiritual man. I prefer to believe in the premise that we are called to love on this journey—I refuse to be motivated or my love be rooted in the selfish idea of getting a return on my investment with eternal life in a field of poppies, but rather because it is the RIGHT THING TO DO. I know only one thing for certain. If you put out love, you will most likely receive love. If you put out good and positive energy, you will most likely receive good and positive energy. It has taken me years to learn the discipline, and I still fall short at times to weed out and exclude those who are negative or hateful from my surroundings. I love people, and I love the thought that every person we encounter has a story. What I have discovered is that if I just take the time and sincerely listen, I can learn from each of them. There is a reason my friends call me "Moeprah"—I'm curious and genuinely interested in hearing other people's stories and life experiences. I know the value of each of them and their plight.

Words just don't seem adequate to describe the privilege and honor it was to watch first-hand as history was being made, and the small number of people who get to call two vice presidents friends is not lost on me. I'm a blessed man. The Jews have a word in Yiddish that is probably my favorite word ever created—"beshirte." Beshirte loosely translated means "when it is meant to be" or fortuitousness. I wholeheartedly believe my journey has been one beshirte moment after another, and I can't wait to discover the next.

I hope my story has reinforced the premise that each of us is unique, special and worthy. Even when we are faced with soul-searching and fundamental challenges in life, we can get our footing and celebrate this magnificent journey. If good fortune and blessings can happen to this chubby, gay, ugly, bald Latino from south Texas, they can most certainly happen to you.

I am now committed to the fact that I will be learning, growing and evolving as a person and spiritual human being until I take my last breath. I'm not sure what happens on that inevitable day, but I'm at peace with not knowing. I do know that I don't want anyone trying to convince, persuade or convert me to believe a certain way—I respect and honor the beliefs of others, and I hope they will do the same to all of us who are comfortable with the unknown. I find fulfillment in simply striving to live life to the fullest, strive to be the best person you can be, and love often and without reservation.

I at least know, or hope I know, what most people will say at my funeral. I leave you with a warning to those who might attend my funeral—I will most likely be at least 15 minutes late, since I tend to function on "gaytino" time!

MOEISMS

1. WORDS MATTER... WE MUST USE WORDS TO BUILD EACH OTHER UP, RAISE ONE ANOTHER UP, CELEBRATE EACH OTHER—NOT DENIGRATE, DIMINISH OR DESTROY.

2. IT'S ABOUT KNOWING YOUR CORE—WHAT DO YOU STAND FOR, WHAT DO YOU BELIEVE, WHAT ARE YOUR PRINCIPLES? THOSE ARE GUIDING PARAMETERS. WITHOUT A CORE OR FOUNDATION, ALL ELSE WILL COLLAPSE!

3. EACH OF US IS A BRAND—NO DIFFERENT THAN THE BRAND THAT IS MARKETED FOR CONSUMPTION OR USAGE. KNOW YOUR BRAND—YOU GET TO CONTROL THE WAY YOU ARE PERECEIVED, RECEIVED AND ACCEPTED. BUILD A BRAND THAT YOU CAN BE PROUD OF AND THAT LASTS THE TEST OF TIME.

4. PUT OUT POSITIVE ENERGY, AND YOU WILL RECEIVE POSITIVE ENERGY.

5. PEOPLE ARE MORE APT TO BUY A PRODUCT OR USE THE SERVICE OF SOMEONE THEY LIKE, ADMIRE AND TRUST.

6. EACH OF US IS WORTHY AND HAS A SEAT AT THE TABLE OF LIFE. TAKE YOUR RIGHTFUL SEAT, AND TAKE IT WITH DIGNITY AND RESPECT FOR YOURSELF AND OTHERS!

7. LAUGH AS OFTEN AS YOU POSSIBLY CAN. AT THE VERY MOMENT IN TIME THAT ONE LAUGHS WITH ANOTHER, ONE ACTUALLY LIKES THEM. IT'S THE MOST POWERFUL TOOL AND GIFT GIVEN TO US.

8. MY GUIDING MANTRA IS TO ALWAYS TRY TO CONNECT WITH MY FELLOW HUMAN BEINGS—SELF-DEPRECATION AND SHARED VULNERABILITY ARE THE QUICKEST ROUTES TO MEANINGFUL CONNECTION.

9. WE ALL HAVE A STORY, CHALLENGE, INSECURITY, DREAM, FEAR AND HOPE... BUILD ON THOSE COMMONALITIES AND CELEBRATE OUR DIFFERENCES!

10. LOVE—JUST SIMPLY LOVE.

ACKNOWLEDGEMENTS

THERE HAVE BEEN SO MANY INCREDIBLE PEOPLE WHO HAVE impacted my life so far and there is no way I could properly or adequately acknowledge each and every one of them, so to anyone who has ever laughed with me, loved me, respected me and enjoyed any aspect of this journey with me, I thank you and love you from the bottom of my heart.

I would be remiss if I did not thank my siblings—Patsy, Luti, Manny (Amy) and Pepper (Bass). You have always been there when I needed you and I know you have my back. I'm so proud of what each of you does on a daily basis to make a difference in people's lives. I also thank you for giving me the greatest gift a gay uncle could ask for----ten amazing nephews and nieces and three great nephews and nieces (and one on the way). I love you all.

I honor and celebrate my nephews and nieces---they are my soul. The depth of my pride and love for them is immeasurable. Each and every one of them and their spouses have picked up the mantle of service and the commitment to leave this world a little better than they found it. I expect great things from each of you and hope that you carry on your Tio Moe's tradition to laugh as often as possible and love without limitation.

I thank Deiv for so many incredible memories and for being the best friend any human could ever need or want.

I thank Magda for her tireless and patient love. She will always be familia.

On the political side, although I express my love and respect for them in the body of this book, I want to acknowledge the profound impact and role they played in my life once again. I thank Al Gore, Tipper Gore, Joe Biden, Jill Biden and the Lieberman family. Each of these people believed in me, trusted me, respected me and loved me. I hope I never let any of you down. They gave me opportunities that most people dream of and that altered the course of my journey in incomparable ways. I respect and I love each of you more than you know.

This book would simply not have been possible without my mentor, brother and friend, Ron Klain. You single-handedly changed the course of my life. You are my Jewish angel. Much of this book is dedicated to you, Ron. Although sad for me, but what a testament to your unselfish and humble service to our nation that I could find not one picture of the two of us together. You have never sought the spotlight yet you have impacted policies, programs, initiatives and political campaigns that have changed the world and our nation. I respect you. I admire you. I love you, my friend.

To all the Longhorn Singers, I love you for providing me with some of the greatest memories and friendships of my life. The chance to perform beside you, make music together, laugh and love with many of you until this day, all bring me comfort, affirmation, a sense of belonging and fulfillment.

I am so absolutely blessed to have some friends that have been in my life for decades, and others, merely days, but each of you makes my heart sing and your love, encouragement and support sustain me. A special shout out to Myra, Christina, Veronica, Gideon, Jeff, Ximena, Sergio, Chris and Andres, Cindy, Jerry and Janet, Brenda and countless others.

I thank my business associates, colleagues and clients—past and present. I have learned so much from each of you and I'm eternally grateful that you have allowed me to walk by your side and succeed together. A special shout out to Zach, Jillian, Helena, Sanjay, Marshall, Sachin, Craig, John and too many others to mention.

I thank each and every one of my teachers from Tony Taylor in first grade, Carol Martinez in fourth grade, the Brumleys and Mrs. Longhofer in high school to Charles Cantu in law school. This book would truly not have been possible without the role that each of you played in my life. Each of you encouraged, guided, educated and enabled me on very crucial and integral steps on this journey of life. A part of this book is dedicated to teachers everywhere and to the role they play in our lives.

I dedicate a part of this book to the memory of Marcia Lieberman. Baba, you left an indelible mark on my heart and soul. I love you more than you will ever know and I'm glad you are reunited with your beloved Henry. Sadly, I have lost all my pictures with Baba and the Lieberman family, but the memories will always remain a fixture in my heart.

I dedicate a part of this book to our active military members, their families, veterans, reservists, national guard, law enforcement officials and firemen. Not a day goes by that I don't realize that we get to enjoy the freedoms we often take for granted because of your unselfish service and sacrifice.

Lastly, I thank my publisher, Justin Sachs, at Motivational Press. You have become my trusted advisor and my business partner, but, above all, you have become my friend. I'm eternally grateful to you for believing in me and this project. My hope is that your new son, Benjamin, and all children everywhere, will live in a world with less hate, full of endless love and in an environment that will provide them the freedom to live their truth and reach their highest potential.